THE MEDITATIONS
OF MARCUS AURELIUS

THE MEDITATIONS

MARCUS AURELIUS ANTONINUS

Translated, with an introduction, by
G. M. A. GRUBE

Hackett Publishing Company, Inc.
Indianapolis/Cambridge

Marcus Aurelius Antoninus: A.D. 121–180

Hackett Publishing Company, Inc.
P.O. Box 44937
Indianapolis, Indiana 46244-0937

www.hackettpublishing.com

First Edition
12 11 10 09 08   13 14 15 16 17 18 19

Cover design by Richard L. Listenberger

Library of Congress Cataloging-in-Publication Data

Marcus Aurelius, Emperor of Rome, 121–180.
    The Meditations.
    Translation of: Meditations.
    Bibliography: p.
    1. Ethics. 2. Stoics. 3. Life. I. Grube, G. M. A.
(George Maximilian Anthony) II. Title.
B580.G77   1983   188   83-22722
ISBN 0-915145-78-2
ISBN 0-915145-79-0 (pbk.)

ISBN-13: 978-0-915145-78-2 (cloth)
ISBN-13: 978-0-915145-79-9 (pbk.)

CONTENTS

THE MEDITATIONS OF MARCUS AURELIUS

INTRODUCTION

MARCUS AURELIUS

When Marcus Aurelius succeeded Antoninus Pius in A.D. 161, it was nearly a hundred years after the dreadful civil wars —the infamous year of the four Emperors—which had followed the death of Nero. The Flavian dynasty—Vespasian, Titus, Domitian—had governed well, though Domitian, impatient of sharing his power with the Senate, had made the imperial power much more personal and dictatorial and had become cruel and tyrannical. The chief victims of this, however, were the Roman aristocrats in Rome itself. After the murder of Domitian in 96, and even that was two generations before Marcus, Rome and the Empire were indeed fortunate in having able and devoted emperors. Thus Marcus came to power in a period of prosperity and comparative peace.

These emperors were childless, and throughout this period the succession was secured by adoption. Old Nerva (emperor 96-98), himself elected by the Senate, adopted Trajan (98-117); Trajan adopted Hadrian (117-138), who in turn adopted Antoninus Pius (138-161), and made doubly sure of avoiding a power vacuum by having Antoninus adopt both Marcus Aurelius and Lucius Verus. Marcus broke with the adoptive method by associating his son with him (and, as Ausonius was to say later: "He inflicted only one injury upon his country, he had a son").[1]

Marcus, then, was not born to the purple, but he was close to the reigning house. For the first seventeen years of his life he received the ordinary education of a young Roman aristocrat. No doubt he was intended for a public career of one sort

---

[1] Ausonius XIV, "On the Twelve Caesars," sec. 17: "Hoc solo patriae, quod genuit, nocuit."

or another, though one doubts whether he looked forward to it. He must have been a serious-minded boy. His name was then Marcus Annaeus Verus, and one likes to remember that the old Emperor Hadrian called him Verissimus—the boy who could not tell a lie. Further, when at the age of eighteen in 139 he received the news of his adoption by Antoninus, which put him in the direct line of succession, it was bad news to him and he received it with sorrow, not elation.[2]

About the time of his adoption his higher education was entrusted to various tutors, the most famous of whom was Marcus Cornelius Fronto. Higher education meant rhetoric, the art of language, with public speaking as the chief mode of expression. Fronto was not only a famous orator, he had definite theories of his own: he tried to revivify the language by a most careful selection of words, with a somewhat precious affectation of archaism and an exaggerated emphasis on similes as almost the chief ornament of prose style. Master and pupil were continually writing to each other, and a good deal of their correspondence, mostly in Latin, is extant. The letters which we have are dated from about 139 to 165, beginning shortly after the adoption, when Marcus was eighteen and a willing pupil, to the time, twenty-six years later, when he was sole ruler of the world. The early letters from Fronto naturally contain more advice on the principles of rhetoric, on what the young man should read, etc., while the tone of the later letters is less magisterial—especially since in 145 Marcus abandoned rhetoric for philosophy. The whole correspondence throws a welcome light on Marcus' character: affectionate to his teacher and his family, capable of enthusiasm especially in the early years, and truly humble always, for the Emperor was, at all ages, far more modest than his teacher!

We can also find traces, from quite early on, of the weariness which crept upon Marcus in his later years, a weariness much increased because he had to spend at official functions so much

[2] Apart from the journal itself and the correspondence with Fronto (see *The Correspondence of Marcus Cornelius Fronto,* tr. and ed. C. R. Haines), we have to rely on a late life and some passages of Dio Cassius.

time he would much rather have spent with his books. He had a special dislike for the gladiatorial shows. Here is part of a letter written in 143, when he was twenty-two:

> It is most kind of you to ask for the hexameters I wrote. I should have sent them to you at once, if I had them with me. But my secretary—you know him, I mean Anicetus—did not pack any of my writings when I started out. The reason is that he knows my weakness and was afraid I might throw them in the fire as I usually do. To be sure, these particular hexameters were in practically no danger, for I may as well confess to my master that I love them. Here I study at night. The daytime is spent in the theater, with the result that I am tired and do less in the evening, and that I'm still sleepy when I get up in the morning. . . .[3]

The note of weariness recurs (still in 143) in this short letter:

> When I am not with you, you read Cato, but I, when you are not with me, have to listen to pleaders till six P.M. I could wish the coming night to be shorter; so much the less time to stay awake, and the sooner to be with you again. Farewell my very dear master. I can hardly breathe, I am so exhausted.[4]

But the young student, with the cares of his position pressing more and more upon him—he had been made Caesar (i.e., heir presumptive) in 139 and was to receive the *tribunicia potestas* which made him junior Emperor and co-ruler, in 147, at the age of 26—became weary of rhetorical tricks, similes and recherché expressions; he turned his back on rhetoric in favor of philosophy about 145, to Fronto's sorrow and annoyance, though it did not affect their personal relations. Perhaps Fronto should not have advised him to read Cato so much, in search of precious words, for he evidently absorbed the spirit of the old Stoic rather than the words only. He also certainly came under the influence of another Stoic at this time, Junius Rusticus.

To understand the importance of this decision to follow phi-

[3] Haines, I, 138.
[4] *Ibid.*, p. 152.

losophy rather than rhetoric, we must appreciate the position of rhetoric in the second century, as well as the appeal of Stoicism. It was the time of the great lecturers, of the affluent professors. Public speakers were in great demand to make key-note addresses on public occasions, games, festivals, or visits of important personages, even of the emperor. "Sophist," which meant a professional rhetorician, was now a title of great honor, and the sons of the best local families would apprentice themselves to some Sophist and travel all over the empire to lecture and display their art. The Sophists were well educated, and the emperors appointed them as state secretaries, as governors of provinces, gave them munificent gifts, and even made them consuls in Rome. Roman nobles sometimes endured with surprising meekness displays of proud insolence on the part of these Greeklings, as when Polemo of Laodicea returned home to Smyrna unexpectedly and turned Antoninus, then proconsul, out of his house in the middle of the night; or Herodes Atticus, the multimillionaire Athenian Sophist, insulted Marcus Aurelius when on trial before his tribunal. Such things could have happened only under the mild philhellenic emperors of the second century; they show, however, the tremendous prestige of these "Sophists," many of whom at one time or another held imperial Chairs of rhetoric at Athens or Rome, and commanded very high fees for their public performances.

So higher education still meant education in rhetoric, as it had in the times of Cicero, Seneca and Quintilian; but for the more intellectual there were also the schools of philosophy. Cicero had unsuccessfully tried to weld rhetoric and philosophy into one system of education nearly two centuries before; and it is not surprising that the serious-minded Marcus Aurelius turned away from rhetoric to philosophy, as his contemporary Lucian turned from rhetoric to satire and founded a new genre, the satirical dialogue.

The philosophy was bound to be Stoicism, and for the practical Roman all other aspects of philosophy were subordinated to ethics. This was in large measure true of all post-Aristotelian philosophies, but both Epicurus and Zeno and their early followers, being in the Greek tradition, still felt an imperative need to base their ethics upon a systematic explanation of the world. Hence their metaphysics, physics, logic, epistemology, theories of sensation and so on; but these other aspects of philosophy were increasingly neglected in the Roman world, especially so under the Empire when Stoicism became more a religion than a philosophy. Epicureanism, in spite of its popularity in the first century B.C., was much less congenial to the Romans.

The Stoics always believed in an all-pervading Logos or Reason which governed the universe. They conceived this Logos to be material and identified it with the rarified form of a kind of divine Fire, which in more or less debased form existed in all things. The whole world periodically, most Stoics believed, returned to fire in a great conflagration or ἐκπύρωσις, and this belief emphasized the unity of the universe. The rational soul, the specifically human part of man, his reason, was a fragment of the universal Logos. It was akin to it, and thus able to understand the divine purpose and to conform to it. And it is this state of mind, this acceptance, which was virtue and which alone brought happiness. Nothing else mattered. All else, health and wealth included, was "indifferent," that is, of no importance at all.

The goal of life, then, was to attain this inner state of mind, this understanding and conformity, and thus to live, as they termed it, "in agreement with nature," ὁμολογουμένως ζῆν τῇ φύσει, or "in accord with nature," κατὰ τὴν φύσιν. To do this willingly was to exercise free will in the true sense. For man had free will; he could fight against the current, but he would then live at odds with Nature's divine and universal purpose, that is, with Reason, both that of the universe and his own. He would thus also live at odds with himself, μαχομένως ζῆν, or at least with the best part of himself, his own truly human nature.

Not even the old Stoics fully worked out the metaphysical

or psychological problems involved. They were always more inclined to dogmatic assertions than to any true philosophic inquiry. The tone of Stoic writings under the early empire, in Seneca and Epictetus as well as in Marcus Aurelius, became increasingly religious. They spoke in terms of divine care and divine providence, and of the Logos or Reason as an almost personal god. All that was not reasonable was irrational; all that was not right was equally wrong. To the old Greek Stoics there were no degrees of right and wrong: you drown as surely, in Cicero's phrase, a foot as a mile under water.[5] This rigidity too was somewhat tempered in Roman times, and more emphasis was placed on progress toward virtue. It became recognized that there is more hope of reaching the surface for those only just below it than for those at the bottom of the sea, so that the ordinary man could derive some encouragement from his progress. Yet the old dogmatism was apt to erupt at any moment, and the old absolutes were never quite given up. The Stoic sage understood the divine purpose perfectly; he saw his duty clearly; nothing or no one could prevent him from discharging it to the best of his ability.

Since only this inner poise mattered, the Stoic, though eager to do his duty, was not to be disturbed by any failure, provided the failure was due to circumstances beyond his control. This strange combination of zeal in action, indifference to results, and distrust of all passions and emotions which might disturb the Stoic's inner poise has been well illustrated by a modern scholar:

> The point of the Stoics was that a thing may serve to give direction to action without being an object of desire. This is obviously true. Supposing you are a servant, sent to fetch a parcel from the post office for your employer; you may be perfectly indifferent as to whether the parcel has arrived or not, yet your whole action in going to the post office, all the consecutive movements of your feet, will be directed by an intention; but if you found that the parcel was not there, you would not be disappointed, and rest satisfied with hav-

[5] Cicero, *De Finibus* III. 48.

ing fulfilled your part of the business. That is a type of the attitude of the Stoic Wise Man towards outward things.[6]

So the Stoic is the servant of the Logos. He will start upon any course of action, as Marcus puts it, conditionally or with reservations, for if circumstances make it impossible to attain his original aim, he will adjust himself to the new circumstances and make *them* a new occasion for the practice of virtue. He will remain unaffected as long as his own disposition, his own state of mind, remains the same, and he continues to act in accord with his own and the divine Reason. He will always perform his human duty and act like a rational human being.

But of course man is not wholly rational. As a living being he shares with all that lives, including animal and plant, what Marcus calls the "breath of life," the πνεῦμα, the life-soul. As an animal, he shares with other animals certain passions and perceptions which belong to the body, and this is the sentient or animal soul. He will care for these less important parts of himself, as he must as long as he lives and perceives, but they must never be allowed to interfere with, or drag down to their own level, his essentially human soul, the reason within him which is but part of the universal Reason. This is τὸ ἡγεμονικόν, the ruling or directing part of himself.[7]

Under the despotic emperors who exacted a sullen obedience from the Senate, Stoicism had been the religion of the opposition; indeed, it was the Stoic temper which made that opposition dangerous. Many chose to die as Stoics rather than live as slaves. For if one's duty was done, then, as the Stoics put it, "The door is open." It is highly significant that the philosophy of the opposition in the first century became that of the Antonine emperors in the second. It is also significant that of the two great Stoics of the second century one was an emperor, and the other, Epictetus, a liberated slave, whom the emperor quotes with respect.

[6] Edwyn Bevan, *Stoics and Sceptics* (Oxford, 1913), pp. 58-59.

[7] This is the divine Reason within him. I have generally translated τὸ ἡγεμονικόν as "the directing mind."

This then was the religion (or philosophy) to which Marcus Aurelius turned for comfort and help in his appointed tasks two years or so before he became co-emperor with Antoninus Pius. Thus he continued for fourteen years more, and when Antoninus died in 161, Marcus succeeded him. Characteristically, he insisted that his adopted brother Lucius Verus share the power with him. Fortunately, perhaps, that pleasant and easy-going young man showed little disposition to shoulder the cares of office. He never tried to dispute Marcus' power, and died in 169, so that Marcus was sole emperor in law for the last eleven years of his reign as he had been in fact since his accession. Marcus' physical health was never strong, and he was not yet sixty when he died, on a military expedition, in A.D. 180.

The peace-loving emperor was forced to wage almost continuous wars throughout his reign. These were due to the unreliability of the vassal kings in the East and the pressure of barbarian migrations in Central Europe. From 161 to 166 there was the Parthian war, technically under the command of the co-emperor Lucius Verus who, however, left the campaigning to his generals and was content to celebrate great triumphs on his return to Rome. It is from this campaign that the returning legions brought back the plague which raged throughout the Empire and is thought by most historians to have so seriously undermined manpower as to be a definite factor in the ultimate decline and fall of Rome. Then barbaric invasions around 166 came as far as Italy itself; Marcus felt compelled to take personal command of the whole campaign along the Danube, and he spent a great deal of his time in camp until he died there. He also had to face a revolt from his chief governor in the East. This led to the new policy that no man should be appointed governor of his native province.

In all these matters Marcus Aurelius showed himself able, energetic, and efficient, but at what cost to himself we can feel as we read his *Meditations*. We can imagine him sitting in his imperial tent in cold Sarmatia beyond the Danube—officers and men asleep around him as he suffered from his customary insomnia—and jotting down the following bitterly ironic words (X. 10):

> A spider is proud when it has hunted down a fly; one man, a hare; another, a sardine in his net; another, piglets; another, bears; another, Sarmatians. Are they not bandits, when you examine their convictions?

The *Meditations* of Marcus Aurelius is a strange, noble, and sad book. The best established title is simply *To Himself;* it is a philosophic diary or journal in which the Emperor, evidently during his later years, jotted down his thoughts and reflections, exhortations and beliefs. That it was written in Greek is not surprising, for Greek was the natural language of philosophy for a bilingual Roman, and most educated Romans were bilingual in the second century. Some sections are just jottings of a few words, or even a string of quotations, as at the end of the seventh book; other sections, as might be expected from a man thoroughly trained in the art of verbal expression, are elaborated and even stylized. Here and there the meaning is obscure, for we cannot be sure what was in Marcus' mind, and an intimate journal is bound to be occasionally cryptic to outsiders. There are very few references to other people after the first book, and no certain references to contemporary events.[8] The thoughts are not in any logical order, and this is very natural, for in a personal journal a thought may be put down one day, then taken up again days, weeks, even months later. Some subjects come up again and again, in no very different words, and a good deal of repetition is inevitable.

Needless to say, scholars have tried to rearrange the Em-

---

[8] Farquharson, *Marcus Aurelius,* p. 123, suggests that the reference to pregnancy at IX. 3 would seem to imply that the Empress was still living; that the references to disloyalty in IX may be an allusion to the treachery of Avidius Cassius; and that the only reference to the Christians, in XI. 3, may have been written at the time of the martyrdoms of Vienne and Lyons, i.e., 177. Obviously this is all very uncertain. Even the reference to the Sarmatians in X. 10 (quoted above) *need* not have been written during that war, though it is the most convincing of these possible references.

peror's thoughts into a more logical sequence, and every such arrangement is inevitably different from every other.[9] This is the kind of insoluble problem for which scholars love to produce solutions, but if one remembers the nature of the work there really is no problem at all. Even the occasional contradiction will surprise no one, and it may well be only apparent. For instance, at the beginning of the eighth book Marcus is obviously concerned with the impossibility of studying philosophy properly for, as he says, his position is against it (VIII. 1), "no time to read" (VIII. 8) and so on. But later (XI. 7) we find him saying that no other position is so conducive to philosophy as that "in which you now find yourself." This seems a flat contradiction. But for all we know the Emperor may have been confined to bed for a while in the second case—what could be more natural? Such an explanation is pure guesswork. We simply do not know the circumstances in which he wrote either passage. He may just have been in a different mood; but, while the statement that his position as emperor kept him from his books appears elsewhere, the statement that this position was most conducive to philosophy is a very unlikely thought at any time—for we remember the rather pathetic reflection: "Wherever it is possible to live, it is possible to live the good life; it is possible to live in a palace; it must therefore be possible to live the good life in a palace" (V. 16), and that other heartfelt, "Do not become Caesarized, or dyed with that coloring . . ." (VI. 30).

But neither slight contradictions nor the lack of the kind of order one expects in a philosophical work (but not in a philosophical journal) is important. Two things, however, *are* important for us to keep in mind if we are to appreciate the unique flavor of the book: firstly, that this is the undisputed master of the Roman world talking to himself, and secondly, that it is to himself that he is talking. The "you" whom he rebukes, castigates, or consoles is not the reader but the Emperor. He might have hoped to use some of the more formal

[9] On these attempts see the Introduction to Farquharson's edition, pp. lviii-lxvi.

passages in some published work which he never had time to write, but the journal as a whole, and most of its sections, were certainly never intended for any eyes but his own.

It is not a book to rush through from cover to cover; rather it is a work to wander in, to pause and to ponder. It is at times repetitive—do we not ourselves often have to repeat our self-exhortations before they are fully effective? Sometimes it is even long-winded, but Fronto's pupil could also use striking language and vivid epigram. Anyone who has fought intolerance and authoritarianism should appreciate the point of (VI. 6): "The best form of defense is not to become like your enemy." Any hot-tempered man has learned to his cost (XI. 18): "How much harder to bear are the consequences of our anger and vexation than were the actions which provoked us to anger and vexation," and all will appreciate the irony of (XII. 27): "The man who swells with pride at his own lack of pride is the hardest of all to tolerate." There are many similar gems.

The first book is different from the others, and a kind of introduction. There Marcus expresses what he owes to his elders, his tutors and his friends. The form of expression is disconcerting: "From grandfather Verus: a kindly and equable disposition," and so on with all the others—as if Marcus meant that he himself had acquired all the virtues of character which he lists. This is clearly not his meaning; he is far too modest to mean anything of the sort. What he does mean is that in these men he had a chance to observe the virtues *they* possessed, to learn their value, and to try to follow their example. He incidentally gives us some striking character sketches, like that of his predecessor and adoptive father Antoninus Pius (sec. 16, with which compare VI. 30). This first book as a whole thus gives us a fairly complete picture of the qualities he admired and of the kind of man he tried to be in practice. The tone is rather more homely and down-to-earth than the more theoretical and philosophical approach of the later books. There is a kind of homely pathos where he says that Alexander the Platonist (12) taught him not to put friends off, when not absolutely necessary, "on the plea of pressing business," or Rusticus (7) "not to walk about the house in full regalia," or Fronto (11) that "aristocrats are somehow lacking in affection." Like most of his countrymen if less than most, Marcus was something of an eclectic. Eclecticism, i.e., taking from every school of philosophy what suits one, appealed strongly to the practical Romans. So Marcus, though a Stoic, was on some points less dogmatic than his Stoic teachers. We shall find him quoting other philosophers, and on the subject of not fearing death he frequently says, "whether we accept atoms or Providence . . . ," that is, either on Epicurean or Stoic premises, there is nothing to fear. Marcus seems almost obsessed at times with the thought of death and the evanescence of all human achievement.

Basically, the Stoic sought happiness in the citadel of his own mind, as did all post-Aristotelian philosophies. He can never forget himself. Yet he is to devote himself, because he lives in accord with the universal purpose, to the good of the whole. There is a deep-rooted contradiction here which was never resolved; both the positive and the negative attitudes will be found in Marcus. We find, on the positive side, that "Men have been born for the sake of one another. Either teach them or bear with them" (VIII. 59). And again (VII. 31): "Love the human race. Follow the divine. . . ." At times this positive attitude is beautifully expressed, as for example (VI. 54): "What does not benefit the swarm is of no benefit to the bee. What does not harm the city cannot harm the citizen . . . " ; and that magnificent passage (V. 6) on the man who does good as naturally as the vine bears its fruit, almost unconsciously, without thought of return. Again and again Marcus tells us that all rational beings, that is, all men, exist for each other's sake.

But there is another side. Since it is the state of the inner self which is virtue, and upon which happiness depends, its integrity must be preserved from all disturbance, and the Stoics were as emphatic as the Epicureans in preaching imperturbability (ἀταραξία), the avoidance of all passions (ἀπαθεία), not least the passion of love, because they destroy self-sufficiency (αὐταρκεία).

A Stoic, like an Epicurean, will do all in his power to help other men, except be emotionally involved. Unlike the Epicurean, however, the Stoic will not withdraw from society; on the contrary, he will play his part to the full—but as a duty, and while preserving his emotional aloofness. This negative attitude is also very clear in Marcus (VIII. 56):

> To my will the will of my neighbor is as irrelevant as is his breath or his flesh. Even though we have come into the world for each other's sake, yet our directing minds each have their own sphere of government. Else my neighbor's evil were my evil, which was not the god's intention, lest it be within another's power to bring misfortune upon me.

Other men may prevent us from doing a particular action, "but they cannot be an obstacle to our desire or our state of mind because of our power of remaining uncommitted and of adaptation" (V. 20), and one must never "be entirely swept along by another's grief" (V. 36, cf. II. 8).

We should recognize that there is truth in this. Man needs to build emotional defenses to retain his sanity, and one who really felt the sufferings of all other men as his own would be of little use either to himself or indeed to the sufferers; but, on the other hand, man also needs emotional motivation, and anyone who intellectually sees injustice all around him but feels no anger or indignation is not likely to do much to correct it. It is largely this lack of emotional motivation, this lack of passion, or rather this setting up of perfect calm as an ideal, which leaves us with an impression of aridity, emptiness, and utter loneliness in the life of the great Stoic Emperor: "how great a weariness there is in living with those who are out of tune with you" (IX. 3). There is something wrong, too, with the advice to "live as on a lonely mountain" (X. 15).

It was a basic dogma of Stoicism that a man's happiness, being this inner state of calm devotion to Reason, was entirely within his power to attain, within his own control, so that nothing which was not within his power was of any real importance. This complete detachment is hardly a very satisfactory basis, one would think, for family life, and one wonders whether, like some other great men, Marcus was unhappy in his own home. In his youthful letters, it is true, he refers to his wife and children with affection, but in his journal, except for the one reference to Faustina as "obedient, affectionate, and simple in her ways" (he certainly does not include her among those from whom he learned anything), there is nothing. Several of his children died in infancy. His surviving son was to be a poor emperor and seems to have been quite unworthy of his father. Faustina herself must remain one of history's minor mysteries. Malicious gossip had much to say about her infidelities, but there is no convincing evidence on the point. At best, however, Marcus in his middle age was probably a lonely man, even in his family life, and one has some sympathy with Faustina, as with Socrates' Xanthippe. Kindly and remote, Marcus must have found it increasingly hard to be interested in individuals, and one can well imagine that some even among his intimates might say to themselves at his death: "Shall we ever be relieved of this schoolmaster? He was not hard on any of us, but I used to see him silently criticizing us" (X. 36).

The philosopher on the throne does his duty, but it is often a wearisome duty. He would so much rather have spent the time with his books. Yet for him, with all his imperial duties to fulfill, study was mere self-indulgence, and he did not often indulge himself. He did once, returning from an Eastern campaign, stop at Athens to attend the lectures of philosophers and give some of his own. We are told that Avidius Cassius, the rebellious Eastern commander who had himself declared emperor at Antioch in 175, admitted that Marcus was indeed a very worthy man, but that he was much too fond of the idle chatter of philosophers to be a good emperor. Many a soldier must have agreed with him.

And yet this dreamer was also trained in practical statesmanship and did not try to impose any theoretical blueprint upon the government of the Empire. "Do not expect Plato's ideal republic; be satisfied with even the smallest step forward, and consider this no small achievement" (IX. 29). He accepted the vast machinery of imperial government as it was, and carried on the traditions of his predecessors. He even made the government, we are told, more centralized, though this, if an evil, was probably necessary. However, in associating his adopted brother with himself as co-emperor with equal powers he created a dangerous and ominous precedent, though with Lucius Verus it did not matter.

There is one feature of his reign which posterity has found hard to understand, namely the persecutions of the Christians which continued during his reign. It seems paradoxical that, in his day and in the following century, it was often the good emperors who persecuted the Christians and the weak emperors who did not care. The Jews were excused from worship of the emperor, but after a time this exemption was withdrawn from the Christians, who were spreading over the whole empire and therefore were potentially far more dangerous. There is only one mention of the Christians in the journal, a contemptuous reference to their ostentatious martyrdom (XI. 3).

It is a difficult question, but we should be clear on certain points. First, that there was no general persecution in the reign of Marcus. Second, the Christian Church had now become a well-organized entity within the Empire and claimed spiritual authority over its members. This seemed intolerable, for the separation of temporal and spiritual powers was utterly at variance with Greek and Roman ideas. Moreover, to refuse a simple ritual such as doing homage in worship to Rome and its emperors seemed treason and sheer obstinacy in a polytheistic civilization. Trajan makes it plain in his correspondence with Pliny that this was all that was required, and even so the Christians were not to be sought out. The very universality of the Church was a challenge to established authority. It seems also that by this time some Christians at least refused military and civil duties, and this, at any rate, no emperor could tolerate. So while he did not initiate persecutions, Marcus did not change the laws which made them possible.

There can be no doubt as to the noble grandeur of the

Stoic ethical ideal, of which we find several full statements (e.g., III. 4, VIII. 55, IX. 1), and we even have a kind of Stoic ten commandments (XI. 18). The complete devotion to the highest in man, to the inner light, to use a modern metaphor, the unquestioning performance of duty without regard to the consequences or what the world may think, the pursuit of the social good, truthfulness, kindliness, understanding and forgiveness for the wrongdoings of others, the rigid control of passions; all this is admirable, even magnificent. Yet always there is a cold wind blowing through the treetops, a remoteness which is due to the perpetual return to the self. "Dig down within yourself, where the source of goodness is ever ready to gush forth, if you always dig deeply" (VII. 59); or again, "Gather yourself within yourself, for the directing mind naturally orders that the righteous man be sufficient unto himself and from this derive his peace" (VII. 28).

This concentration on the self, this self-examination, self-exhortation, is characteristic not only of Marcus but of Stoics generally, and in Roman Stoics it came dangerously close to self-nagging. From the days when the old Greek Stoics insisted that every deviation from the right was equally wrong, Stoicism always lacked a sense of proportion, and also, I fear, a sense of humor. Marcus will exhort himself to get up in the morning with the same moral earnestness as to take command of an army. The flaw in Stoicism, which refused to recognize any mean between absolute virtue and absolute vice, led them to ignore any half-way house between the world society (which the Empire nearly was) and the individual, or between the individual and the all-pervading Logos or Reason. But man needs stepping stones, and he needs fellowship, emotional as well as intellectual, with his associates. Stoicism, dedicated to the self-sufficiency of the individual, just failed to provide this sense of fellowship, though it came very close to doing so when it spoke of the brotherhood of man, the common weal, the common purpose of the universe. But brothers cannot live unto themselves alone and remain brothers.

The search for happiness within the individual's own soul is not peculiar to Stoicism; indeed its most beautiful expression is found in the famous passage at the beginning of the second book of Lucretius' *De Rerum Natura:*

> 'Tis sweet, when the storm rages out at sea,
> Safely ashore to watch another toil. . . .

This withdrawal of the individual is characteristic of all post-Aristotelian Greek philosophies, in strong contrast to the Platonic philosophy of man as a social animal. The later Greek philosophers were fundamentally asocial; though, as we have seen, Stoicism at least had its positive side. It was natural enough for the Greeks to preach the withdrawal of the individual once the precarious balance between man as a citizen and man as an individual was lost with the disappearance of the city-states as independent nations, at the close of the fourth century. The Greeks, for all their ideas on the federation of nations and their many experiments, never in practice solved the urgent social-political problem of establishing the supra-city-state political and social structure which the times demanded. The Romans, when their day came, did solve that problem, and the sword was not their only instrument. But by that time "captive Greece had conquered her rude conqueror," as Horace put it,[10] and the Romans, enslaved as they were to the Greeks in matters of thought, never developed a philosophy of life commensurate with their practical achievement. They merely tried to apply Greek ideas to their very different Roman world. No wonder something was lacking.

The lack is felt in Marcus Aurelius, but it was not a personal failure so much as a failure of the world in which he lived. He was not a happy man, obviously, but he was a very great one; he not only had high ideals but he lived up to them as few men have been capable of doing. His journal is not a cheerful book, but it is a noble book, and at the same time very personal and very touching. It is not often that we can

10 Horace, *Epistles* II. 1. 156-57.

share the innermost thoughts of a man of his quality in his terribly responsible position. We can, I believe, find much in it to help us in our own lives, in our own thoughts and actions; for we too live in a world where the idealist who works to realize his ideals may well, like Marcus, at times feel very tired and very close to despair. Stoicism may not have made him happy, but it gave him faith, strength, and courage, and it kept despair at bay.

SELECTED BIBLIOGRAPHY

TRANSLATIONS

Farquharson, A. S. L. *The Meditations of the Emperor Marcus Antonius.* 2 vols. Oxford, 1944. This is the standard edition in English, with introduction, critical text, translation, and full commentaries on text and background.

Haines, C. R. *The Communings with himself of Marcus Aurelius, Emperor of Rome.* ("Loeb Classical Library.") Harvard, 1916; reprinted 1953. Contains Introduction, text, and translation, with short notes.

Leopold, I. H. *Marcus Aurelius Imperator ad se ipsum.* ("Oxford texts" series.) Oxford, 1908.

Trannoy, A. I. *Marc-Aurèle, Pensées.* ("Budé" series.) Paris, 1953. Introduction by A. Puech.

The *Meditations* have frequently been translated. The old translation of Mcric Casaubon, first published in 1635, still has a good deal of merit and was republished early in this century by Dent in the "Temple Classics" series. Jeremy Taylor's translation (1701) was long popular; among others George Long's (1862) has often been reissued, and one should mention John Jackson's in "The World Classics" series (1911), which has also been frequently reprinted.

THE LIFE OF MARCUS AURELIUS

Farquharson, A. S. L. *Marcus Aurelius, his Life and his World.* Oxford, 1951. Contains a number of essays by Farquharson published posthumously, edited by D. A. Rees, but the work was never completed.

Haines, C. R. *The Correspondence of Marcus Cornelius Fronto.* 2 vols. ("Loeb Classical Library.") Harvard, 1919; reprinted 1955. Contains text and translation of the extant letters exchanged between Marcus Aurelius and his old tutor. Most of them are in Latin, a few in Greek.

Hayward, F. H. *Marcus Aurelius, a Saviour of Men.* London, 1935.

Sedgwick, H. D. *Marcus Aurelius, a Biography.* New Haven, 1921.

STOIC PHILOSOPHY

Arnold, E. V. *Roman Stoicism.* Cambridge, 1911; reprinted New York, 1958.

Bevan, E. *Stoics and Sceptics.* Oxford, 1913.

Edelstein, L. *The Meaning of Stoicism.* Cambridge, MA, 1966.

Hicks, R. D. *Stoics and Epicureans.* New York, 1910.

Higginson, T. W. *Epictetus, The Enchiridion.* ("Library of Liberal Arts," No. 8.) New York, 1948. A translation of the Manual of Epictetus, containing his principal doctrines.

Long, A. A., (ed.) *Problems in Stoicism.* London, 1971. A collec-- tion of critical essays.

Long, A. A. *Hellenistic Philosophy.* London, 1974.

Oates, W. J. (ed.) *The Stoic and Epicurean Philosophers.* New York, 1940. Contains translations of the works of Epicurus (C. Bailey), Lucretius (H. A. T. Munro), Epictetus (P. E. Matheson), and Marcus Aurelius (Long).

Oldfather, W. A. *Epictetus, The Discourses as reported by Arrian.* 2 vols. ("Loeb Classical Library.") Harvard, 1925; reprinted 1956. Text and translation of the conversations of Epictetus.

Pohlenz, M. *Die Stoa.* 3rd ed., Göttingen, 1964 (2 vols.).

Rist, J. M. *Stoic Philosophy.* Cambridge, 1969.

Rist, J. M. (ed.) *The Stoics.* Berkeley, Los Angeles, and London, 1978. A collection of critical essays.

White, N. P. *The Handbook of Epictetus*. Indianapolis, 1983. Contains introduction, translation, and notes.

HISTORICAL BACKGROUND

Bury, J. B. *The Student's Roman Empire*. London, 1913.

The Cambridge Ancient History. Vol. XI. Cambridge, 1936. See especially ch. 9, "The Antonines," by W. Weber, and ch. 17, by F. H. Sandbach.

Dill, Samuel. *Roman Society from Nero to M. Aurelius*. London, 1905; reprinted ("Meridian Books"), Cleveland, Ohio, 1956.

The Selected Bibliography has been updated in 1983 by DONALD J. ZEYL

THE MEDITATIONS
OF MARCUS AURELIUS

NOTE ON THE TEXT

The text of *The Meditations* is not in very good condition; in detail it is often obscure, and in places corrupt beyond emendation. I have followed the text of Farquharson's edition (Oxford, 1944), and any significant departure is stated in the notes.

G. M. A. GRUBE

BOOK I

1. From grandfather Verus: [1] a kindly and equable disposition.

2. From the reputation of my father and what I remember of him: [2] self-respect and manly behavior.

3. From my mother: [3] piety, generosity, to avoid not only evil deeds but evil thoughts; to live simply without any display of wealth.

4. From my great-grandfather: not to have attended popular schools, but to have good teachers at home, and to know that one should spend freely on such things.

5. From my tutor: [4] not to be a Green or a Blue partisan at the races, or a supporter of the lightly armed or heavily armed gladiators at the Circus; endurance and frugality; to do one's own work and not be a busybody; not to welcome slanderous gossip.

6. From Diognetus: to avoid frivolous enthusiasms; to distrust what miraclemongers and magicians say about charms, exorcising spirits, and the like; not to keep quails for cockfights or get excited about such sports; to tolerate plain-speaking; to be at home in philosophy and attend the lectures first of Baccheius, then of Tandasis and Marcianus; [5] to write dialogues when still a boy; to want to sleep on a pallet or on hides, and other such things as the Greeks are trained to.

[1] By this form of expression which continues throughout the book, Marcus does not mean that he had acquired these and all other qualities, but that he had the opportunity to observe them. See Introd., p. xvii.

[2] Marcus' father, Annius Verus, died before the boy was fifteen.

[3] Domitia Lucilla, granddaughter of L. Catilius Severus, who is referred to in the next section.

[4] The name seems to have dropped out, and we cannot be sure who is meant.

[5] Nothing is known of these three philosophers.

7. From Rusticus: to come to realize that one's character needs correction and training; not to be sidetracked into the pursuit of the rhetoric of the Sophists, not to write about one's theories or preach one's little sermons, not to show off by posing as a trained philosopher or a benefactor; to abstain from rhetoric and poetry and clever talk; not to walk about the house in full regalia or do things of that sort; to write letters in a simple style like the letter Rusticus himself wrote to my mother from Sinoessa; to be ready to resume friendly relations with those who have annoyed or wronged you as soon as they themselves want to resume them; to read with care and not to be satisfied with a general understanding of the subject or agree easily with superficial chatter; an acquaintance with the works of Epictetus, of which he lent me his own copy.

8. From Apollonius: [6] to be free with a certainty beyond all chance, not to look to anything else but Reason even for a moment; to be the same man always, when in great pain, at the loss of a child, or during a long illness; clearly to realize from his living example, that the same man can be very much in earnest and yet relaxed; not to be impatient in explanation; observing a man who obviously considered his experience and skill in communicating his ideas the least of his accomplishments; learning how to accept apparent favors from one's friends, without being humiliated by them or unfeelingly returning them.

9. From Sextus: [7] kindliness; the pattern of a household governed by the father; understanding what it means to live according to nature; genuine dignity; affectionate consideration for one's friends' feelings; to be tolerant of the uncultured and of those whose opinions are not thought out; to be accommodating to all men, so that they found his company more agreeable than any flattery, and those who enjoyed it considered the occasion one worthy of respect; a clear grasp and methodical valuation of those doctrines which are essential to

[6] Apollonius of Chalcedon.
[7] Sextus of Chaeronea.

life; to show no trace of anger or any other passion, to be quite unperturbed and yet very affectionate; to praise without fuss, and to be very learned without ostentation.

10. From Alexander the grammarian: [8] to refrain from reproach, not to rebuke those who utter a barbarism or solecism or make some error in pronunciation, but neatly to introduce what they should have said when one answers them or adds a suggestion or proof on the very same subject, without discussing the verbal expression—or in some other way to remind them of the correct usage.

11. From Fronto: to note what it means for a ruler to be envious, unreliable, or to act a part: how, generally speaking, those we call aristocrats are somehow lacking in affection.

12. From Alexander the Platonist: only rarely and when unavoidable to say or to write to someone, "I am too busy," and not in this way, on the plea of pressing business, to continually excuse ourselves from performing the duties we owe to those who live with us.

13. From Catulus: [9] not to ignore a friend's criticism even if it happens to be unreasonable but to try to restore his usual friendliness; to speak of one's teachers with heartfelt respect, as in what is recorded about Domitius [10] and Athenodotus; to be genuinely fond of children.

14. From Severus: love of family, love of truth, love of justice; to have known, because of him, Thrasea, Helvidius, Cato, Dion,[11] and Brutus; to grasp the idea of a Commonwealth with the same laws for all, governed on the basis of equality and free speech, also the idea of a monarchy which prizes the liberty of its subjects above all things; from him also, a vigorous consistency in the appreciation of philosophy; beneficence, eager generosity, and optimism; confidence in the affection of one's friends, and frankness toward those who incurred his

---

[8] Alexander of Cotiaeum.
[9] Nothing is known of this Catulus.
[10] Presumably Domitius Afer.
[11] Presumably Dio Chrysostomos.

censure; so that his friends had no need to guess at his desires or intentions, but they were obvious.

15. From Maximus: self-control, not to be easily influenced; to be of good cheer in illness and in all other misfortunes: a well-balanced disposition, sweet temper, dignified bearing; to perform one's appointed task without resentment; the fact that all men trusted him to mean what he said and to do whatever he did without malice; to be immune to surprise, undaunted, never hasty, dilatory or at a loss, never to be downcast or sneering or again angry or suspicious, but generous, forgiving, and truthful; to give the impression of one who cannot be corrupted rather than of one who has been reformed. Also, that no one thought himself slighted by him, or would venture to consider himself his superior. To be gracious in. . . .[12]

16. From my father:[13] to be gentle, and to stick unwaveringly to decisions taken after due investigations; not to take an empty pride in what are considered honors; to love work and to persevere in it; to listen to those who have something to contribute to the common good; to give to each man impartially what he deserves; to know from experience when there is need for exertion, and when for relaxation; to put a stop to homosexual passions for young men; to be considerate: he excused his friends from attending him at dinner continually and from the obligation of accompanying him on a journey, yet he remained equally friendly with those whom other engagements compelled to remain behind; to investigate carefully such matters as came before Council: he would persevere in this, did not give up easily, and was never satisfied with first impressions; to keep one's friends, and never be fickle or infatuated; to be master of oneself in everything, and to be of good cheer; to look far ahead, and to manage everyday affairs without dramatics. Public acclamations and every form of flattery were checked in his reign.

To watch always over the essential needs of the empire, to

---

[12] A few words are lost at this point.
[13] That is, his adopted father, the emperor Antoninus Pius.

allocate its resources, and to tolerate criticism in these matters. To be free from superstitious fear of the gods and not to court the favor of men by being obsequious or seeking to please the mob; to be sober and steadfast in all things; never to lack good taste nor to pursue novelty for its own sake; to use the comforts of life without arrogance or apology when fortune provides them in abundance, so as to enjoy them when they are available, without making a practice of it, and not to feel the lack of them when they are not; not to cause anyone to call one a sophist or an imposter or a pedant but a man of mature experience, one who is above flattery and able to manage his own affairs and those of others.

Beside this, to honor genuine philosophers, not reproaching the other kind but not being influenced by them; to be sociable and agreeable, but not to excess, moderately careful of one's own bodily health, not like a man in love with living or with a view to beautifying oneself, yet at the same time not despising one's body, so that by paying attention to details oneself, one very rarely needs medical help, medicines, and slaves; most important, to yield without malice to those who have special ability, be it in expression, in the study of laws or customs or other matters, and to give them help in their pursuits, so that each of them may achieve distinction in his own field; to act in all things in accordance with the traditions of our fathers without making this very thing one's aim, namely to be noted for preserving the traditions of our fathers; not to be always chopping and changing, moving from place to place and from one course of action to another; after the most violent headaches to return to one's customary tasks with renewed vigor; there were not many things which could not be mentioned to him, for his secrets were few and far between, and exclusively concerned with matters of state; reasonable moderation in providing public spectacles, in carrying out public works, in the distribution of bounty and the like, for he was a man who acted with an eye to what needed to be done, not to the glory he could get from doing it.

He was not one to indulge in baths at all times of the day,

nor was he fond of building; he did not give much thought to food, to the texture or color of his clothes, or to physical beauty. His clothes came from his country residence at Lorium. There are many stories of his mode of life at Lanuvium, of his treatment of the apologetic tax-gatherer at Tusculum,[14] and of that kind of behavior.

His manner was never harsh, inexorable or violent; no one could say it was heated. All business was allotted its calculated time as if he were a man of leisure; and every item was dealt with in calm, orderly, vigorous, and consistent manner, within its allotted time. What we are told of Socrates could be suitably applied to him: that he could either abstain from, or enjoy, those pleasures which most men are too weak to abstain from, or to enjoy without complete surrender to them.

Strength of character, self-control, and sobriety, both in abstention and in enjoyment, belong to the man who has a perfect and invincible spirit such as Maximus displayed in his illness.[15]

17. From the gods: to have had good grandparents, good parents, a good sister, good teachers, a good household, good relations and friends, and almost everything; that I did not happen to give offense to any one of them although I had a disposition that might have led me to do so, and I owe it to the beneficence of the gods that no combination of circumstances was to test me in this respect; that I was not to be brought up any longer with my grandfather's common-law wife; that I preserved my adolescence and did not become a man before the proper time but even took a little longer; that I was subjected to the rule of a father who was to rid me of all vanity and to make me realize that it is possible to live in a palace without feeling the need of bodyguards or striking clothes or chandeliers or statues or other such vanities, but to reduce oneself very nearly to the status of a private citizen

[14] This anecdote is not known, and the text here is uncertain.

[15] The Maximus here referred to is presumably the same as the subject of section 15. See Biographical Index.

without thereby abasing oneself or neglecting the duties of
leadership for the common good.

That I had a brother whose moral character could rouse me
to care for my own, and whose affection and respect brought
me joy; that my children have not been dull or physically de-
formed; that I did not progress more rapidly in rhetoric, poetry
or other such pursuits, which might have held me back from
my proper duties if I had been conscious of easy proficiency in
them; that I could quite early raise my tutors to honorable
offices which I thought they desired, and not leave them hoping
that, as they were still young, I might do so later; that I have
known Apollonius, Rusticus, and Maximus; that I often had
a clear picture in mind of what it means to live in accord with
nature, so that, in so far as it lay with the gods, their gifts,
help, and inspiration, nothing stops me from living in accord
with nature, and if I still fall short of this it is through my
own fault, and because I have not paid attention to the re-
minders, one might almost say the teachings, of the gods; that
my bodily health,has been adequate so far for my kind of life;
that I had no sexual relations with Benedicta or Theodotus,[16]
and that even later when erotic passion came to me, I retained
my health; that, though I was often angry with Rusticus, I did
nothing excessive which I should have repented; that, while
my mother was fated to die young, she yet lived her last years
with me; that whenever I wished to help someone in poverty
or need, I was never told that I did not have the means to do
so, and that I myself never fell into similar need and had to
accept help from another; that my wife was so obedient,
affectionate and artless; that I could easily obtain suitable
tutors for my children; that I was granted help through
dreams, especially on how to avoid spitting blood or feeling
dizzy, and by the oracle at Caieta: [17] "as you will treat your-

16 Nothing is known of these persons. They were probably household
slaves.

17 Presumably Marcus consulted the oracle of Apollo at Caieta and "as
you will treat yourself" was part of the oracular response. Perhaps he asked

self"; that, though I longed for philosophy, I did not fall in
with any Sophist or withdraw from active life to analyze literary compositions or syllogisms, or busy myself with questions
of natural science, for all these things need the help of the
gods and of Fortune.

---

what his chances were of a happy life and the priest of Apollo replied
that this depended on him and how he "treated himself," i.e., how far he
lived in accord with the best in himself and his life was governed by his
reason or directing mind.

BOOK II

1. Say to yourself in the morning: I shall meet people who are interfering, ungracious, insolent, full of guile, deceitful and antisocial; they have all become like that because they have no understanding of good and evil. But I who have contemplated the essential beauty of good and the essential ugliness of evil, who know that the nature of the wrongdoer is of one kin with mine—not indeed of the same blood or seed but sharing the same mind, the same portion of the divine—I cannot be harmed by any one of them, and no one can involve me in shame. I cannot feel anger against him who is of my kin, nor hate him. We were born to labor together, like the feet, the hands, the eyes, and the rows of upper and lower teeth. To work against one another is therefore contrary to nature, and to be angry against a man or turn one's back on him is to work against him.

2. Whatever it is which I am, it is flesh, breath of life, and directing mind.[1] The flesh you should despise: blood, bones

---

[1] The opposition between the higher and lower parts of man is expressed in various ways. Sometimes as a mere opposition of body and soul, which roughly equates reason with soul. More strictly, however, soul is of three kinds: the breath of life or life-soul, which man shares with all living things including plants; the perceptive part of the soul which man shares with animals (here called the flesh), and the reason which belongs only to man, and therefore may be said to *be* man as distinguished from all other living things. Here and in the next section these reflections on the soul are curiously interwoven with the thought that he himself has no time for study. The connection of thought seems to be that, as man is truly his reasonable part or directing mind, so each directing mind has its own place and duty in the universe, and in Marcus' own case this requires him to fulfill all the duties of his position as emperor, and not to indulge his longing for philosophy.

There is an implied contradiction between contempt for the body and admiration for all the works of nature, of which the body must be counted as one, but the contradiction is implicit in any kind of religious asceticism, not only Stoic.

and a network woven of nerves, veins and arteries. Consider too the nature of the life-breath: wind, never the same, but disgorged and then again gulped in, continually. The third part is the directing mind. Throw away your books, be no longer anxious: that was not your given role. Rather reflect thus as if death were now before you: "You are an old man, let this third part be enslaved no longer, nor be a mere puppet on the strings of selfish desire; no longer let it be vexed by your past or present lot, or peer suspiciously into the future."

3. The works of the gods are full of Providence. The works of Chance are not divorced from Nature or from the spinning and weaving together of those things which are governed by Providence. Thence everything flows. There is also Necessity and what is beneficial to the whole ordered universe of which you are a part.[2] That which is brought by the nature of the Whole, and preserves it, is good for every part. As do changes in the elements, so changes in their compounds preserve the ordered universe. That should be enough for you, these should ever be your beliefs. Cast out the thirst for books that you may not die growling, but with true graciousness, and grateful to the gods from the heart.

[2] The relation between these different forces is not always clearly worked out. The supreme governing Reason (also called the Soul of the universe) was early identified with Zeus, as in the hymn of Cleanthes in the third century B.C., and when the word god is used in the singular it refers to this. Stoicism, however, did not do away with polytheism; the other gods were thought of as fragments of this Reason directing different parts of the universe, and heavenly bodies were also spoken of as gods. Providence or Foresight (*pronoia*) is a natural attribute of the gods. The nature of the Whole is another aspect of the divine soul or souls, the working out of their providence in the world as we know it. Necessity is one aspect of this, which corresponds to what we might call the laws of matter, and although matter and the material can be an obstacle to perfection, it ultimately obeys, though not necessarily in the life of an individual or any one event. Chance seems a contradiction of all this: it is, however, properly used to mean the accidental and unintended concomitants of certain natural processes (III. 2). Men will also attribute to Chance anything of which they do not understand the causes.

The Greek word for the universe, *kosmos*, implies an ordered universe.

4. Remember how long you have delayed, how often the gods have appointed the day of your redemption and you have let it pass. Now, if ever, you must realize of what kind of ordered universe you are a part, of what kind of governor of that universe you are an emanation, that a time limit has now been set for you and that if you do not use it to come out into the light, it will be lost, and you will be lost, and there will be no further opportunity.

5. Firmly, as a Roman and a man should, think at all times how you can perform the task at hand with precise and genuine dignity, sympathy, independence, and justice, making yourself free from all other preoccupations. This you will achieve if you perform every action as if it was the last of your life, if you rid yourself of all aimless thoughts, of all emotional opposition to the dictates of reason, of all pretense, selfishness and displeasure with your lot. You see how few are the things a man must overcome to enable him to live a smoothly flowing and godly life; for even the gods will require nothing further from the man who keeps to these beliefs.

emotional burnout?

6. You shame yourself, my soul, you shame yourself, and you will have no further opportunity to respect yourself; the life of every man is short and yours is almost finished while you do not respect yourself but allow your happiness to depend upon the souls of others.

7. Do external circumstances to some extent distract you? Give yourself leisure to acquire some further good knowledge and cease to wander aimlessly. Then one must guard against another kind of wandering, for those who are exhausted by life, and have no aim at which to direct every impulse and generally every impression, are foolish in their deeds as well as in their words.

8. A man is not easily found to be unhappy because he takes no thought for what happens in the soul of another; it is those who do not attend to the disturbances of their own soul who are inevitably in a state of unhappiness.

9. Always keep this thought in mind: what is the essential

nature of the universe and what is my own essential nature? How is the one related to the other, being so small a part of so great a Whole? And remember that no one can prevent your deeds and your words being in accord with nature.

10. Theophrastus speaks as a philosopher when, in comparing sins as a man commonly might, he states that offenses due to desire are worse than those due to anger, for the angry man appears to be in the grip of pain and hidden pangs when he discards Reason, whereas he who sins through desire, being overcome by pleasure, seems more licentious and more effeminate in his wrongdoing. So Theophrastus is right, and speaks in a manner worthy of philosophy, when he says that one who sins through pleasure deserves more blame than one who sins through pain. The latter is more like a man who was wronged first and compelled by pain to anger; the former starts on the path to sin of his own accord, driven to action by desire.

11. It is possible to depart from life at this moment. Have this thought in mind whenever you act, speak, or think. There is nothing terrible in leaving the company of men, if the gods exist, for they would not involve you in evil. If, on the other hand, they do not exist or do not concern themselves with human affairs, then what is life to me in a universe devoid of gods or of Providence? But they do exist and do care for humanity, and have put it altogether within a man's power not to fall into real evils. And if anything else were evil they would have seen to it that it be in every man's power not to fall into it. As for that which does not make a man worse, how could it make the life of man worse? [3]

Neither through ignorance nor with knowledge could the nature of the Whole have neglected to guard against this or correct it; nor through lack of power or skill could it have committed so great a wrong, namely that good and evil should come to the good and the evil alike, and at random. True, death and life, good and ill repute, toil and pleasure, wealth and poverty, being neither good nor bad, come to the good

[3] For the independence of the individual, see Introd., pp. xii-xiii, xviii-xix.

and the bad equally. They are therefore neither blessings nor evils.

12. How swiftly all things vanish; in the universe the bodies themselves, and in time the memories of them. Of what kind are all the objects of sense, especially those which entice us by means of pleasure, frighten us by means of pain, or are shouted about in vainglory; how cheap they are, how contemptible, sordid, corruptible and dead—upon this our intellectual faculty should fix its attention. Who are these men whose voice and judgment make or break reputations? What is the nature of death? When a man examines it in itself, and with his share of intelligence dissolves the imaginings which cling to it, he conceives it to be no other than a function of nature, and to fear a natural function is to be only a child. Death is not only a function of nature but beneficial to it.

How does man reach god, with what part of himself, and in what condition must that part be?

13. Nothing is more wretched than the man who runs around in circles busying himself with all kinds of things—investigating things below the earth, as the saying goes—always looking for signs of what his neighbors are feeling and thinking. He does not realize that it is enough to be concerned with the spirit within oneself and genuinely to serve it. This service consists in keeping it free from passions, aimlessness, and discontent with its fate at the hands of gods and men. What comes from the gods must be revered because of their goodness; what comes from men must be welcomed because of our kinship, although sometimes these things are also pitiful in a sense, because of men's ignorance of good and evil, which is no less a disability than to be unable to distinguish between black and white.

14. Even if you were to live three thousand years or three times ten thousand, remember nevertheless that no one can shed another life than this which he is living, nor live another life than this which he is shedding, so that the longest and the shortest life come to the same thing. The present is equal for

all, and that which is being lost is equal, and that which is being shed is thus shown to be but a moment. No one can shed that which is past, nor what is still to come; for how could he be deprived of what he does not possess?

Therefore remember these two things always: first, that all things as they come round again have been the same from eternity, and it makes no difference whether you see the same things for a hundred years, or for two hundred years, or for an infinite time; second, that the longest-lived or the shortest-lived sheds the same thing at death, for it is the present moment only of which he will be deprived, if indeed only the present moment is his, and no man can discard what he does not have.

15. "All is but thinking so." The retort to the saying of Monimus the Cynic is obvious, but the usefulness of the saying is also obvious, if one accepts the essential meaning of it insofar as it is true.

16. The human soul violates itself most of all when it becomes, as far as it can, a separate tumor or growth upon the universe; for to be discontented with anything that happens is to rebel against that Nature which embraces, in some part of itself, all other natures. The soul violates itself also whenever it turns away from a man and opposes him to do him harm, as do the souls of angry men; thirdly, whenever it is overcome by pleasure or pain; fourthly, whenever it acts a part and does or says anything falsely and hypocritically; fifthly, when it fails to direct any action or impulse to a goal, but acts at random, without purpose, whereas even the most trifling actions must be directed toward the end; and this end, for reasonable creatures, is to follow the reason and the law of the most honored commonwealth and constitution.

17. In human life time is but a point, reality a flux, perception indistinct, the composition of the body subject to easy corruption, the soul a spinning top, fortune hard to make out, fame confused. To put it briefly: physical things are but a flowing stream, things of the soul dreams and vanity; life is

but a struggle and the visit to a strange land, posthumous fame
but a forgetting.

What then can help us on our way? One thing only: philosophy. This consists in guarding our inner spirit inviolate and
unharmed, stronger than pleasures and pains, never acting
aimlessly, falsely or hypocritically, independent of the actions
or inaction of others, accepting all that happens or is given as
coming from whence one came oneself, and at all times awaiting death with contented mind as being only the release of
the elements of which every creature is composed. If it is
nothing fearful for the elements themselves that one should
continually change into another, why should anyone look with
suspicion upon the change and dissolution of all things? For
this is in accord with nature, and nothing evil is in accord
with nature.

BOOK III

1. We must consider not only this, namely that our life is spent day by day and that a smaller portion of it remains, but we must also take into account that it is doubtful whether, if a man live long, his mind will retain an equal and sufficient capacity for the understanding of events and for that theoretical contemplation which contributes to the experience and knowledge of things divine and human. For if dotage sets in, a man's weakness does not lie in his respiratory or digestive systems, in his imagination, his desires or the like; the lack is in his power to make proper use of his capacities, to gauge his various duties precisely, to analyze his impressions, even to decide whether he should leave this life, and all such matters as require trained thought. We must therefore hasten on, not merely because death comes closer every day, but because our understanding of events and our ability to act on such understanding come to an end before we do.

2. We should also observe things like these: that the incidental results of natural phenomena have some charm and attractiveness. For example, when a loaf of bread is being baked, some parts break open, and these cracks, which are not intended by the baker's craft, somehow stand out and arouse in us a special eagerness to eat; figs, too, burst open when they are very ripe, and the very closeness of decay adds a special beauty to olives that have ripened on the tree. The same is true of ears of wheat as they bend to the ground, of the wrinkles of a lion's brow, of the foam flowing from a boar's mouth, and of many other things. Looked at in themselves they are far from attractive, but because they accompany natural phenomena they further adorn them and attract us. As a result, the man of feeling and deeper understanding of the phenomena in Nature as a whole will find almost all these incidentals pleasantly contrived. He will look with as much

pleasure upon the gaping jaws of actual wild beasts as upon representations of them in painting or sculpture. He will see a kind of fulfillment and freshness in the old, whether man or woman; he will be able to look upon the loveliness of his own slave boys with eyes free from lust.

Many such things will not appeal to everyone, but only to the man who has come to be genuinely at home with Nature and her works.

3. Hippocrates cured many diseases and then died of disease himself. The Chaldeans foretold many deaths and then their own death overtook them. Alexander, Pompey, and Julius Caesar many times utterly destroyed whole cities, cut down many myriads of cavalry and infantry in battle, and then came the day of their own death. Heraclitus, as a natural philosopher, spoke at great length of the conflagration of the universe; he was a victim of dropsy, covered himself with cow dung, and died. Democritus was killed by vermin, and Socrates by another kind of vermin.[1] What does it mean? You embarked, you sailed, you came to harbor. Disembark now; if to another life, nothing is void of gods even there; if to insensibility, you will cease to endure pleasures and pains, cease to serve a bodily vessel as much the worse as its servant is superior to it, for the latter is Mind and inner Spirit while the former is but earth and gore.

4. Do not waste what remains of your life thinking about other people, if these thoughts bear no relation to some common good. Why deprive yourself of some other task in order to do this: to imagine what so-and-so is doing and why, what he is saying, thinking or contriving, and other such things as keep you from observing your own directing reason. The sequence of your thoughts should avoid vain and random fancies, interference and malice above all. You must accus-

---

[1] This story of death by vermin (literally lice) is not told elsewhere of Democritus, though it is found about other philosophers. Marcus does not usually express himself so brutally about the human race, for of course the vermin killing Socrates are human. The form of expression is probably due to the desire of repeating the word vermin.

tom yourself to think only such thoughts as would enable you, when asked what you are thinking, frankly to answer "this" or "that." Your answer would make clear that all your thoughts were simple and kind, as becomes a social being who is not concerned with pleasures or any sensuous delights of the imagination, or with rivalry, slander, suspicion, or anything else which you would blush to reveal that you had in mind.

Such a man no longer puts off joining the company of the best; he is priest and servant to the gods, he has the right relationship with the spirit established within him, which makes him a man uncorrupted by pleasure, unwounded by pain, untouched by violence, immune to evil and a contender for the greatest prize, which is: not to be overcome by any passion, to be deeply steeped in justice; to welcome one's lot and portion with one's whole soul; rarely, and then only when the common good makes it imperative, to imagine what another may be saying, doing, or thinking.

It is only with what is part of himself that a man can act, and only his own fate, assigned to him from the whole of Nature, which he can at all times reflect upon; his actions he makes beautiful; his fate, he is convinced, is good, for every man carries his appointed fate with him, and it carries him along. He also keeps in mind that all that is endowed with Reason is akin, and that while it is in accordance with man's nature to care for all men, he must not be swayed by the opinion of all men, but only by that of those who live in agreement with nature. As for those who do not live in such agreement, he will have it in mind always what kind of men they are at home and abroad, by night and by day, and what tainted company they keep. Praise from such men he will think of no account, for they are not content even with themselves.

5. Let not your actions be unwilling, selfish, uncritical, or in the grip of conflicting passions, Let not affectation dress up your motives, be not a man of too many words or busy with other people's affairs. The god within you should be the protector of a being who is a man, of mature years, a statesman,

a Roman and a ruler, who has taken up his post as might one who is at ease while awaiting the call to retreat from life, who needs no oath or the testimony of any human witness. Let him be of good cheer, not requiring any external service or rest which other men can give. One should *be* right, not be set right.

6. If you find in human life something better than justice, truth, self-control, courage, something better, in a word, than that your mind should be contented with itself when it makes you act according to the rule of Reason and contented with your destiny in what is allotted to you without any choice— if, I say, you see something better than this, then turn to it with all your soul and enjoy this best which you have found. But if nothing is shown to be better than the divine spirit itself which is established within you, the spirit which brings your private impulses under its dominion, scrutinizes your impressions and, as Socrates said, withdraws itself from the emotions of sense; a spirit which subordinates itself to the service of the gods and takes thought for men; if then you find all other things unimportant and paltry in comparison, then give no place to anything else in your thoughts, for if you incline and lean toward anything else you will no longer be able without distraction to give the place of honor to that good which is peculiarly your own.

It is not lawful for anything different—be it the praise of men, offices of power, wealth, or the enjoyment of pleasures— to stand in the way of what is reasonable and for the common good. All these things, even if for a while they seem to accord with the good life, suddenly overwhelm one and lead one astray. Do you, I say, in freedom and simplicity choose the better part and cling to it. "But the better is the advantageous." If you mean to your advantage as a reasonable being, give heed to it, but if you mean to your advantage as an animal creature, say so, and keep to your decision without vanity. Only see to it that your examination of the question be without danger to yourself.

7. Never esteem as beneficial to yourself what will compel

you to break faith, to abandon self-respect, to hate, suspect, or curse anyone, to dissemble, to long for anything which requires the privacy of walls and curtains. A man who has chosen the side of the mind and spirit within him and has become a worshipper of their excellence does not indulge in dramatics or lamentations; he needs neither solitude nor crowds; above all, he does not lead a life of pursuit and retreat. It does not matter at all to him whether he will have his soul within the body for a longer or a shorter time; if the time has come to depart, he will do so as easily as he would perform any other orderly and reverent action. His one care throughout life is that his mind should not adopt a way of life alien to a thinking and social being.

8. In the mind of a man whose appetites have been chastened and purified you will find nothing abscessed, festering or suppurating. His appointed day of death does not overtake an unfinished life, as if a tragic actor were leaving the stage before completing the drama or playing through his part. Moreover, you will find nothing servile or boastful, nothing compulsive or arbitrary, nothing that calls for an accounting, nothing hidden.

9. Revere your faculty of thought; everything depends upon it, in order that there be no thought in your directing mind which is at odds with nature or incompatible with your status as a reasonable being. It is your faculty of thought which ensures that you be not prone to stumble into error, but at home among men and a follower of the gods.

10. Discard all else; cling to these few things only. Remember, moreover, that each man lives only this present moment; as for the rest, either it has been lived in the past or it is but an uncertain future. Small is the moment which each man lives, small too the corner of the earth which he inhabits; even the greatest posthumous fame is small, and it too depends upon a succession of short-lived men who will die very soon, who do not know even themselves, let alone one who died long ago.

11. To the above advice one thing must yet be added: always to define or describe to oneself the object of our perceptions so that we can grasp its essential nature unadorned, a separate and distinct whole, to tell oneself its particular name as well as the names of the elements from which it was made and into which it will be dissolved.

Nothing is more conducive to high-mindedness than the capacity to examine methodically and with truth everything that one meets in life, and to observe it in such a manner as to understand the nature of the universe, the usefulness of each thing within it, and the value of each in relation to the Whole and in relation to man as a citizen of that Whole, the greatest city of which other cities are but households. What is this which now makes an impression on me? What elements went into its making? How long is it meant to last? And again, what virtue can be employed in dealing with it—be it gentleness or courage, or truthfulness, loyalty, simplicity, self-sufficiency and the rest?

Therefore one must say in each case: This comes from the gods, or this is in accordance with the pattern of the fates' weaving or with the structure of events and chance; that other comes from a man of the same tribe and kin and community as I, but one who does not know what, for him, is according to nature, whereas I do know. Therefore I deal with him in accordance with the law of our common nature, kindly and justly, but at the same time I aim at his true deserts in the dispensing of things in themselves neither good nor evil.

12. If you perform the task before you and follow the right rule of reason steadfastly, vigorously, with kindness; if you allow no distraction but preserve the spirit within you in its pure state as if you had to surrender it at any moment; if you concentrate on this, expecting nothing and shirking nothing, content to do any natural action which is at hand, heroically truthful in every word you utter, you will lead the good life. There is no one who could prevent you.

13. As doctors always keep their equipment and instruments

ready at hand in case they are suddenly called upon to treat a patient, so do you keep ready your doctrines in order to understand things both divine and human and to perform every action, even the slightest, as one who remembers the bonds which unite the two, for you can do nothing well on the human level without reference to the divine, or vice versa.

14. No more vague wanderings. You are not likely to read your memoranda, your histories of Greece and Rome, or the extracts from books which you put aside for your old age. Hasten then to the end, discard vain hopes, and if you care for yourself at all, rescue yourself while you still may.

15. They do not know the full significance of thieving, sowing, buying, keeping quiet, seeing what needs to be done—a significance not perceived by the eye but by another kind of sight.

16. Body, soul, mind. Sense perceptions are of the body, desires of the soul, doctrines of the mind. To receive sense impressions belongs also to cattle; the jerks on the leading strings of desires are felt also by wild beasts, by male prostitutes, by a Phalaris or a Nero; the direction of the mind in what they believe to be their duty is accepted by unbelievers, traitors, and those who commit any crime behind closed doors. If then all else is shared by those mentioned, there remains as characteristic of the good man that he loves and welcomes whatever happens to him and whatever his fate may bring, that he does not pollute the spirit established within his breast or confuse it with a mass of impressions and imaginings, but preserves it blameless, modestly following the divine, saying nothing but what is true, doing nothing but what is just.

If all men refuse to believe that he lives a simple, self-respecting and cheerful life, he will feel no resentment against anyone, nor will he be diverted from the path which leads him to the end of life; and to this he must come pure, calm, ready for release, and attuned without compulsion to his fate.

BOOK IV

1. The attitude of that which rules within us toward outside events, if it is in accord with nature, is ever to adapt itself easily to what is possible in the given circumstances. It does not direct its affection upon any particular set of circumstances to work upon, but it starts out toward its objects with reservations,[1] and converts any obstacle into material for its own action, as fire does when it overpowers what is thrown upon it. A small flame might be quenched by it, but a bright fire very rapidly appropriates to itself whatever is put upon it, consumes it and rises higher because of these obstacles.

2. Let no action be done at random, or in any other way than in accordance with the principle which perfects the art.

3. Men seek retreats for themselves in country places, on beaches and mountains, and you yourself are wont to long for such retreats, but that is altogether unenlightened when it is possible at any hour you please to find a retreat within yourself. For nowhere can a man withdraw to a more untroubled quietude than in his own soul, especially a man who has within him things of which the contemplation will at once put him perfectly at ease, and by ease I mean nothing other than orderly conduct. Grant yourself this withdrawal continually, and refresh yourself. Let these be brief and elemental doctrines which when present will suffice to overwhelm all sorrows and to send you back no longer resentful of the things to which you return.

For what is it you resent? The wickedness of men? Reflect on the conclusion that rational beings are born for the sake of each other, that tolerance is a part of righteousness, and that men do not sin on purpose. Consider how many men have been hostile and suspicious, have hated and waged war, and

1 For the meaning of this phrase see Introd., p. xiii.

then been laid out for burial or reduced to ashes. Desist then. Do you resent the portions received from the whole? Consider the alternatives afresh, namely "Providence or atoms," [2] and how many proofs there are that the universe is like a city community. Are you still affected by the things of the body? Reflect that the mind, once it has freed itself and come to know its own capacities, is no longer involved in the movements of animal life, whether these be smooth or tumultuous. For the rest, recall all you have heard about pain and pleasure, to which you have given assent.

Does paltry fame disturb you? Look how swift is the forgetting of all things in the chaos of infinite time before and after, how empty is noisy applause, how liable to change and uncritical are those who seem to speak well of us, how narrow the boundaries within which fame is confined. The whole earth is but a point in the universe, and how small a part of the earth is the corner in which you live. And how many are those who there will praise you, and what sort of men are they?

From now on keep in mind the retreat into this little territory within yourself. Avoid spasms and tensions above all; be free and look at your troubles like a man, a citizen and a mortal creature. Among the foremost things which you will look into are these two: first, that external matters do not affect the soul but stand quietly outside it, while true disturbances come from the inner judgment; second, that everything you see has all but changed already and is no more. Keep constantly in mind in how many things you yourself have witnessed changes already. The universe is change, life is understanding.

4. If we have intelligence in common, so we have reason which makes us reasoning beings, and that practical reason which orders what we must or must not do; then the law too

[2] That is, either the universe is directed by Reason and Providence, as Marcus and the Stoics believed, or it is a mechanical conglomeration of atoms which scatter at death, as the Epicureans thought. These are the two alternatives Marcus considers here and elsewhere, e.g., IV. 27.

is common to us and, if so, we are citizens; if so, we share a common government; if so, the universe is, as it were, a city—for what other common government could one say is shared by all mankind?

From this, the common city, we derive our intelligence, our reason and our law—from what else? Just as the dry earth-element in me has been portioned off from earth somewhere, and the water in me from the other element, the air or breath from some other source and the dry and fiery from a source of its own (for nothing comes from what does not exist or returns to it), so also then the intelligence comes from somewhere.

5. Death, like birth, is a mystery of nature. The one is a joining together of the same elements into which the other is a dissolving. In any case, it is nothing of which one should be ashamed, for it is not incompatible with the nature of a rational being or the logic of its composition.

6. Their nature inevitably required that they behave in this way. He who wants this not to be wants a fig tree not to produce its acrid juice. In any case remember this: within a very short time both you and he will have died, and soon not even your name will survive.

7. Discard the thought of injury, and the words "I have been injured" are gone; discard the words "I have been injured," and the injury is gone.

8. What does not make a man worse does not make his life worse, and does him no injury, external or internal.

9. The nature of the universally beneficial has inevitably brought this about.

10. "Everything which happens, is right." Examine this saying carefully and you will find it so. I do not mean right merely in the sense that it fits the pattern of events, but in the sense of just, as if someone were giving each his due. Examine this then as you have begun to do, and, whatever you do, do it as a good man should, as the word good is properly understood. Safeguard this goodness in your every action.

11. Do not think the thoughts of an insolent man or those he wishes you to think, but see things as they truly are.

12. You should always be ready for two things, first, to do only what reason, as embodied in the arts of kingship and legislation, perceives to be to the benefit of mankind; second, to change your course if one be present to put you right and make you abandon a certain opinion. Such change, however, should always result from being convinced of what is just and for the common good, and what you choose to do must be of that nature, not because pleasure or fame may result from it.

13. "You are endowed with reason." "I am." "Then why not use it, for, if it fulfills its proper function, what more do you want?"

14. You exist but as a part of the Whole. You will disappear into the Whole which created you, or rather you will be taken up into the creative Reason when the change comes.

15. Many grains of incense on the same altar; one was cast earlier, the other later, but it makes no difference.

16. Within ten days you will seem a god to the same men who now think you a beast or an ape, if you go back to your principles and the worship of Reason.

17. Live not as if you had ten thousand years before you. Necessity is upon you. While you live, while you may, become good.

18. How much ease he gains who does not look at what his neighbor says or does or thinks, but only at what he himself is doing in order that his own action may be just, pious, and good. Do not glance aside at another's black character but run the straight course to the finishing line, without being diverted.

19. The man who thrills at the thought of later fame fails to realize that every one of those who remember him will very shortly die, as well as himself. So will their successors, until all memory of him is quenched as it travels through the minds of men, the flame of whose life is lit and then put out. But suppose those who will remember you to be immortal and the

memory of you everlasting; even so, what is it to you? And I do not mean that praise is nothing to you when dead, but what is it to you while you live, except insofar as it affects your management of affairs? For now you inopportunely neglect nature's gift of virtue while you cling to some other concern.

20. All that has any beauty at all owes this to itself, and is complete in itself, but praise is no part of it. Nothing becomes either better or worse for being praised, and I mean this to apply also to things more commonly called beautiful, such as works of nature or works of art. As for the truly beautiful, it has no need of anything further, any more than does law, or truth, or kindness or reverence. Which of these things is made beautiful by praise or destroyed by censure? Does an emerald become less beautiful if it is not praised? What of gold, ivory, purple, a lyre, a dagger, a little flower or a bush?

21. If souls live on, how has the air of heaven made room for them through eternity? [3] How has the earth made room for such a long time for the bodies of those who are buried in it? Just as on earth, after these bodies have persisted for a while, their change and decomposition makes room for other bodies, so with the souls which have migrated into the upper air. After they have remained there for a certain time, they change and are dissolved and turned to fire as they are absorbed into the creative Reason, and in this way make room for those additional souls who come to share their dwelling place. Thus might one answer on the assumption that souls live on.

One should not, however, consider only the multitude of bodies that are buried thus, but also take into account the multitude of animals eaten every day by us and by other ani-

[3] One may imagine the question to be asked by an Epicurean, since they did not believe in immortality. Marcus' answer is that just as the matter of physical bodies is used to make other things, so the soul is reabsorbed into the Logos. The distinction at the end of the section is between physical matter and soul as the causal principle, though strictly speaking the Stoics believed the soul itself to be a more subtle kind of matter.

mals, how great is the number thus consumed and in a manner buried in the bodies of those who eat them. Yet there is room for them nevertheless because they are transformed into blood and changed into air and fire.

Where lies the investigation of the truth in this matter? In distinguishing between the matter and the cause.

22. Do not wander aimlessly, but give every impulse its just due, and in every sensation preserve the power of comprehension.

23. Everything which is in tune with you, O Universe, is in tune with me. Nothing which happens at the right time for you is early or late for me. Everything, O Nature, which your seasons produce is fruit to me. All things come from you, exist in you, and will return to you. If he could say: "Beloved city of Cecrops," [4] will you not say: "Beloved city of Zeus"?

24. "Do but little, if you would have contentment." [5] Surely it is better to do what is necessary, as much as the reason of one who is by nature a social creature demands, and in the manner reason requires it to be done. This will not only bring the contentment derived from right conduct, but also that of doing little, since most of our words and actions are unnecessary and whoever eliminates these will have more leisure and be less disturbed. Hence one should on each occasion remind oneself: "Surely this is not one of the necessary actions?" One should eliminate not only unnecessary actions but also unnecessary imaginings, for then no irrelevant actions will follow.

25. Make trial of how the life of the good man turns out for you, of the man who is glad of the share he receives from the Whole and satisfied if his own action be just and his own disposition kindly.

26. You have seen those things; look also at these: do not disturb yourself, achieve simplicity in yourself. Someone does

---

[4] The phrase "beloved city of Cecrops" (i.e., Athens) was used by Aristophanes. Marcus means that the universe is as obviously a community as Athens was.

[5] An Epicurean saying.

wrong? The wrong is to himself. Something has happened to you? It is well. From the beginning all that happens has been ordained and fated for you as your part of the Whole. In a word, life is short; we must therefore derive benefit from the present circumstances with prudence and with justice. Be sober and relaxed.

27. Either a universe with order and purpose or a medley thrown together by chance, but that too has order. Or can there be order of a kind in your inner world, but no order in the Whole, especially as all things are distinguished from one another, yet intermingle, and respond to each other?

28. A character that is black, effeminate, obstinate, beast-like, subhuman, childish, stupid, repulsive, vulgar, money-grubbing, tyrannical.

29. If the man who does not understand the truths embodied in the universe is a stranger in it, no less a stranger is he who does not understand what happens in the world of sense. An exile is he who flees from social principle; blind, who keeps the eye of his mind closed; a beggar, who has need of another and does not possess within himself all that is of use in life. A tumor on the universe is he who cuts himself off in rebellion against the logic of our common nature because he is dissatisfied with his lot, for it is that nature which brought it about, as it also brought you about. He is but a splinter off the community who separates his own soul from that of all rational beings, which is one.

30. One man practices philosophy though he has no tunic, another, though he has no book. Yet another man is half naked: "I have no bread," says he, "but I stay on the path of Reason." I have the nurture provided by learning, but I do not stay on that path.

31. Treasure what little you have learnt and find refreshment in it. Go through what remains of your life as one who has wholeheartedly entrusted all that is his to the gods and has not made himself either despot or slave to any man.

32. Consider, for the sake of argument, the times of

Vespasian; you will see all the same things: men marrying, begetting children, being ill, dying, fighting wars, feasting, trading, farming, flattering, asserting themselves, suspecting, plotting, praying for the death of others, grumbling at their present lot, falling in love, hoarding, longing for consulships and kingships. But the life of those men no longer exists, anywhere. Then turn to the times of Trajan; again, everything is the same; and that life too is dead. Contemplate and observe in the same way the records of the other periods of time, indeed of whole nations: how many men have struggled eagerly and then, after a little while, fell and were resolved into their elements. But above all call to mind those whom you yourself have witnessed vainly struggling because they would not act in accord with their own nature and cling to it, and be satisfied with it. It is necessary thus to remind ourselves that every action requires the attention we give it to be measured according to its value, for if you do not dwell more than is fitting upon things of lesser importance, you will not impatiently give up the struggle.

33. Words of old in common usage now sound strange; so the names of men much sung of old are strange today. Camillus, Caeso,[6] Volesus, Dentatus, a little later Scipio and Cato, too, then even Augustus, then even Hadrian and Antoninus. For all things fade and quickly become legend, soon to be lost in total forgetting. This I say of those who shone in wondrous glory; as for other men, they are no sooner dead than "unknown, unheard of." [7] But in any case, what is eternal remembrance? It is altogether vain.

What is it which should earnestly concern us? This only: a just mind, actions for the common good, speech which never lies, and a disposition which welcomes all that happens as necessary and comprehensible, as flowing from a like origin and source.

[6] We do not know who this Caeso is. For the others, see Biographical Index.

[7] The words are quoted from *Odyssey* I. 242, where Telemachus laments his father Odysseus' disappearance.

34. Surrender yourself willingly to Clotho to help her spin whatever fate she will.

35. All is ephemeral, the one remembering and the one remembered.

36. Observe continually all that is born through change, and accustom yourself to reflect that the nature of the Whole loves nothing so much as to change existing things and to make similar new things. All that exists is in a sense the seed of what will be born from it, but you regard as seeds only those which are cast into the earth or the womb. But that is too unenlightened.

37. You will now soon be dead, but you are not yet simple, nor undisturbed, nor free of the suspicion that harm may come to you from outside, nor gracious to all, nor convinced that the only wisdom lies in righteous action.

38. Look to their directing minds, observe the wise: what they avoid and what they pursue.

39. Whether a thing is bad for you does not depend upon another man's directing mind, nor upon any turn or change in your environment. Upon what then? Upon that part of you which judges what is bad. Let it make no such judgment and all is well. Even when that which is closest to it, your body, is cut, burnt, suppurating or festering, let the judging part of you keep calm. That is, let it judge that anything which happens equally to a bad and a good man cannot be either bad or good; for that which happens both to the man who lives in disaccord with nature and to the man who lives in accord with it cannot itself be either in accord with nature or contrary to it.

40. One should continually think of the universe as one living being, with one substance and one soul—how all it contains falls under its one unitary perception, how all its actions derive from one impulse, how all things together cause all that happens, and the nature of the resulting web and pattern of events.

41. You are a little soul carrying a corpse, as Epictetus says.[8]

42. There is no evil in things in process of change, nor any good in things resulting from change.

43. Time is a river of things that become, with a strong current. No sooner is a thing seen than it has been swept away, and something else is being carried past, and still another thing will follow.

44. Everything that happens is as customary and understandable as the rose in springtime or the fruit in summer. The same is true of disease, death, slander and conspiracy, and all the things which delight or pain foolish men.

45. What happens next is always intimately related to what went before. It is not a question of merely adding up disparate things connected by inevitable succession, but events are logically interdependent. Just as the realities are established in tune with one another, so, in the world of sense, phenomena do not occur merely in succession, but they display an amazing affinity with one another.

46. Always remember the words of Heraclitus [9] that "the death of earth becomes water and the death of water becomes air, and that of air, fire, and so back again." Remember also what he says about the man who has forgotten whither the road leads. And "men are at odds with that with which they are in most constant touch, namely the Reason" which governs all; and again, "those things seem strange to them which they meet every day"; and "we must not act and speak as if asleep," for even then we seem to act and speak. And that one should not accept things "like children from parents" simply because they have been handed down to us.

47. If a god were to tell you that you will die tomorrow, or at any rate the day after, you would not make much of the

[8] This fragment of Epictetus (26) is preserved here only. Cf. below, IX. 24.

[9] For the sayings of Heraclitus quoted in this section see Diels, *Fragmenta der Vorsokratiker*, namely fragments 36, 76, 71, 72, 73 and 74 under Heraclitus.

difference between the day after and tomorrow—not unless you were altogether ignoble, for how short is the time between!

So now consider that the difference between the last possible year and tomorrow is no great matter.

48. Think continually how many doctors have died who often knit their brows over their dying patients, how many astrologers who had foretold the deaths of others as a matter of importance, how many philosophers who had discoursed at great length on death and immortality, how many heroic warriors who had killed many men, how many tyrants who had used their power over men's lives with terrible brutality, as if immortal themselves. How often have not whole cities died, if I may use the phrase, Helike, Pompeii, Herculaneum,[10] and innumerable others. Go over in your mind the dead whom you have known, one after the other: one paid the last rites to a friend and was himself laid out for burial by a third, who also died; and all in a short time. Altogether, human affairs must be regarded as ephemeral, and of little worth: yesterday sperm, tomorrow a mummy or ashes.

Journey then through this moment of time in accord with nature, and graciously depart, as a ripened olive might fall, praising the earth which produced it, grateful to the tree that made it grow.

49. Be like a rock against which the waves of the sea break unceasingly. It stands unmoved, and the feverish waters around it are stilled.

"I am unfortunate because this has happened to me." No indeed, but I am fortunate because I endure what has happened without grief, neither shaken by the present nor afraid of the future. Something of this sort could happen to any man, but not every man can endure it without grieving. Why then is this more unfortunate than that is fortunate? Would you call anything a misfortune which is not incompatible with man's nature, or call incompatible with the nature of man

[10] The city of Helike in Achaea was suddenly destroyed in 373 B.C. when it sank into the sea. In 79 B.C. the eruption of Vesuvius in Campania destroyed Pompeii and Herculaneum.

that which is not contrary to his nature's purpose? You have learned to know that purpose. What has happened can then in no way prevent you from being just, great-hearted, chaste, wise, steadfast, truthful, self-respecting and free, or prevent you from possessing those other qualities in the presence of which man's nature finds its own fulfillment. Remember in the future, when something happens which tends to make you grieve, to cling to this doctrine: this is no misfortune, but to endure it nobly is good fortune.

50. It is simple but effective in helping you despise death to go over the list of those who clung to life a long time. What advantage have they over those who died prematurely? Anyway, wherever are they? Caedicianus, Fabius, Julianus, Lepidus,[11] and any other there may be. They assisted at the burial of many and then were buried themselves. In any case, the difference in time is short; among what great troubles we endure it to the end, in what poor company, in how puny a body! Is it not rather a burden? See the abyss of past time behind you and another infinity of time in front. In that context, what difference is there between one who lives three days and a Nestor who lives for three generations?

51. Hasten always along the short road—the road in accord with nature is short—so that you always say and do what is most wholesome. To keep this aim before one frees a man from the wearisome troubles of military service, management of all kinds of affairs, and affectation.[12]

[11] It seems that the names in this section refer to men whom Marcus himself had known and who had died, not to characters in early Roman history.

[12] The meaning of this section is obscure. Marcus seems to mean that if we realize how short life is we shall not labor so hard, or get so weary of our various duties, realizing that they will last only a short time. He obviously cannot mean that we shall refuse to perform these duties, which would be contrary to his Stoic creed.

BOOK V

1. When, in the early morning, you are reluctant to get up, have this thought in mind: "I rise to do a man's work. Am I still resentful as I go to do the task for which I was born and for the sake of which I was brought into the world? Was I made to warm myself under the blankets?" "But this is more pleasant." Were you born for pleasure, to feel things, and not to do them? Do you not see plants, sparrows, ants, spiders and bees perform their proper task and contribute, as far as in them lies, to the order of the universe? Yet you refuse to perform man's task and you do not hasten to do what your nature demands. "But one must also rest." Certainly, I agree. Nature, however, has set a limit to rest, as it has to eating and drinking, and you go on resting beyond that limit, beyond what is sufficient. Not so with your actions, which remain well within the limits of what you could do.

You do not love yourself. If you did, you would certainly love your own nature and its purpose. Other men love their own craft and wear themselves out in the performance of it without bath or food. You love your own nature less than the metalworker loves the art of working metals, the dancer the art of dancing, the money-lover his money or the lover of glory his precious reputation. They, in their passionate eagerness, sacrifice food and sleep to promote the objects of their passion, whereas you believe public affairs to be less important and less deserving of devotion.

2. How easy it is to banish and blot out every disturbing or uncongenial impression from the mind and at once to achieve a perfect calm.

3. Judge yourself worthy of all speech and action which is in accord with nature, and do not let the reproaches or talk which may follow on the part of others divert you. If it was well done or well said, do not depreciate yourself. The others

have their own mind to direct them, and follow their own
desires. Do not look aside to them, but go straight on, following your own nature and that of the Whole; the path is one
and the same for both.

4. I travel my path as it leads through what is in accord
with nature until I fall by the wayside and find rest, breathing
my last into that air from which day by day I draw breath,
while my body falls to join the earth from which my father
received the seed, my mother the blood, my nurse the milk
which were mine, that earth from which day by day for so
many years I have been fed and watered as I stepped upon it,
and which I have made use of for so many things.

5. Men cannot admire you for cleverness. Very well, but
there are many other qualities of which you cannot say: "I
have not the natural gift." Display then those virtues which
are entirely within your power: sincerity, dignity, endurance
of pain, indifference to pleasure, contentment, self-sufficiency,
kindliness, freedom, simplicity, common sense, and magna-
nimity. Do you not see how many virtues can be yours which
do not admit the excuse of lack of inborn talent or of inapti-
tude? And yet you are still willing to be inferior in them. Does
any lack of natural talent compel you to grumble, to be grasp-
ing, to toady, to denounce your poor body, to curry favor, to
be vulgarly complacent, or to be always undecided in your
mind? No, by the gods. You could have rid yourself of all
these faults long ago and only been convicted, if such is indeed the case, of being a somewhat dull and slow learner. And
even a man's mind must be trained, unless he is satisfied to
encourage his slowness of wit and to take pleasure in it.

6. One man, when he has done a good deed, is ready also to
put down in his accounts the gratitude due to him. Another
is not prepared to do this, but privately he thinks that something is owed to him, and he is aware of what he has done. A
third man does not, in a sense, even know what he has done,
but he is like a vine which has produced its grapes and seeks

nothing beyond having once borne its proper fruit. Like the horse who has raced, the dog who has followed the scent, the bee who has made honey, this man who has done good does not know it, but turns to the next task, as the vine turns to produce grapes again in due season. One should therefore be among those who do good, in a sense, unconsciously. "Yes, but one must be aware of the fact itself, for," he tells us, "it is the part of the social man to perceive that he is acting for the common good, and to want, surely, his neighbor to know it." What you say is true, but you misunderstand what is now said; for this reason you will be one of those I previously mentioned; they too are misled by a reasonable conviction. If you want to understand the nature of our argument, be not afraid that it may lead you to neglect some socially useful action.

7. A prayer of the Athenians: "Rain, rain, beloved Zeus, upon the fields and the plains of the Athenians." Thus simply we should pray, like free men, or not pray at all.[1]

8. Just as we say that Asclepius prescribed horseback riding for someone, or cold baths, or walking barefoot, so we say that the nature of the Whole has prescribed disease for someone, or lameness, or loss of limb, or anything else of the same kind. In the first statement the word "prescribed" is used with much the same meaning as in the second. Asclepius orders something as contributing to health, and what happens to every individual is somehow ordered for him as contributing to his destiny. We say these things "happen" to us as builders say that square stones "happen" to fit into walls and pyramids when in a certain position. For there is one universal harmony, and, as out of all bodies the universe is composed into one harmonious body, so out of all the causes the one harmonious fated cause is perfected. Even the quite unenlightened grasp my meaning for they say: "This was his lot." Thus this was allotted to him

---

[1] The meaning seems to be that we should pray for something which is good for the whole community, and not only for ourselves. The point of praying like free men is that one should not cringe or pray in fear, but be ready to accept whatever the gods may send.

and ordered for him. Let us then accept these happings as we accept those prescriptions of Asclepius, for some of them too are harsh, but we welcome them, hoping for health.

You must consider the doing and perfecting of what the universal Nature decrees in the same light as your health, and welcome all that happens, even if it seems harsh, because it leads to the health of the universe, the welfare and well-being of Zeus. For he would not have allotted this to anyone if it were not beneficial to the Whole.[2] No sort of nature brings anything to pass which does not contribute to that which it governs. You must therefore welcome with love what happens to you, for two reasons: first, because it happens to you, is prescribed for you, is related to you, a fate spun for you from above by the most venerable of causes; second, because whatever comes to an individual is a cause of the well-being and the welfare, indeed of the permanence, of that which governs the Whole. For the whole universe is maimed if you sever anything whatever from the coalescing continuity of its parts, and the same is true of its causes. Yet you do sever something, insofar as it is in your power to do so, whenever you are discontented, and in a way you destroy that continuity.

9. Do not give up in disgust and impatience if you do not succeed in acting from right principles in every particular, but return to your principles after taking a fall, and be glad that most of your actions are more worthy of a man. Love that to which you are returning; do not return to philosophy as to a reproachful tutor, but as the victim of ophthalmia returns to his sponges and white of egg, or a sick man to his compresses and poultices. In this way you will show that obedience to Reason is no burden, but even a relief. Remember that philosophy only wants such things as your nature wants; it was you who wanted something else not in accord with nature. What gives more delight than this accord? And is it not

2 Farquharson (I. 329) rightly notes that Marcus does *not* say that the suffering is actually good for the individual concerned, but only that it contributes to the harmony of the Whole.

through delight that pleasure deceives us? But consider whether there is not more delight to be found in high-mindedness, freedom, simplicity, and piety. What gives more delight than wisdom itself, when you think how reliable and consistent is the capacity to know and to follow up that knowledge?

10. The truth of things is, we might say, so wrapped in obscurity that not a few philosophers, and those not the least, have thought it altogether beyond understanding, while the Stoics themselves think it hard to grasp. Every judgment we make is fallible, for where is there an infallible man? Next, consider the things themselves, how short-lived they are, how unimportant, how they can be acquired by a male prostitute, a whore, or a thief. After this, consider the characters of your associates, of which even the most charming is hard to tolerate, not to mention that a man finds it hard to tolerate his own character. In such darkness and dirt, in such a changing stream of existence, time, movement, and moving things, I do not see what there is to be honored or even to be seriously pursued at all. On the contrary, one should exhort oneself to await natural dissolution, not to chafe at delay but to find refreshment in these reflections only: first, "Nothing will happen to me which is not in accord with the nature of the Whole," and second, "It is possible for me to do nothing contrary to the god and the spirit within me, for there is no one who can compel me to do so."

11. To what end am I using my soul? One should ask oneself this on all occasions, and inquire: "What occupies that part of me which they call the directing mind? What kind of soul do I have now? Is it that of a child, a youth, a woman, a tyrant, a tame animal, a wild beast?"

12. What kinds of things the majority believe to be "goods" you might know from this: if one were thinking of the possession of what are truly goods, such as wisdom, self-control, justice and courage, then with those in mind one could no

longer listen to the saying, "Your goods are so many," [3] for it no longer applies. On the other hand, if a man is thinking of what the majority believe to be goods, he will hear it out and readily accept the words of the comic poet as appropriate. So even the majority is conscious of the difference, for otherwise the saying would not have given offense and been criticized, while at the same time we accepted it as a strikingly appropriate witticism when applied to the possession of wealth and the benefits of luxury and reputation. Go on from this to ask whether we should prize and consider as blessings things of which, when we think of them, it can appropriately be said that their possessor has no place in which to relieve himself.

13. I have been made out of that which is cause and that which is matter. Neither of these will be destroyed into nonexistence just as neither was made out of the nonexistent. Therefore when the change comes every part of me will be assigned its place in that which is a part of the universe, and that part again will change into another part, and so on indefinitely. It is by a change of this kind that I came to be, and so with my parents, and so on in another infinite sequence. Nothing prevents one's saying this, even if the world is governed in a sequence of appointed cycles of time.[4]

14. Reason and the art of reasoning are powers sufficient unto themselves and to their works. They start from the appropriate premise and make their way to the end set before them—they travel to the proposed conclusion; this is why such

[3] Marcus is here quoting an old proverb, also quoted by Menander, applying to the rich man whose house is so full of treasures that there is no place left to relieve oneself. It was obviously well known; Marcus actually refers to it by quoting only the first few and last words. A similar comment on ostentatious wealth is found in the story told of Diogenes the Cynic who spat in his host's face as he could find no other place in the house to spit.

[4] Marcus means that one can speak of change in endless sequence even if, as some Stoics believed, there were periodic conflagrations at which times the world returned to the state of original "fire," for after every period the process would begin again.

actions are called "straight," with reference to the straightness of the road.

15. A man should give no heed to those things which do not belong to man's portion as a human being. They are not demanded of man, the nature of man does not proclaim them, nor do they make his nature more complete. Man does not find his end in them, nor the means to that end, which is the good. Moreover, if any of these things were proper to man, then neither contempt for them nor neglect of them could be proper to him; we would not praise one who shows he does not need them; nor could one who is not at his best in dealing with one or other of them be a good man, if these things were good. As it is, the more a man does without them or allows himself to be deprived of them, the better man he is.

16. The kind of thoughts you frequently have will make your mind of the same kind, for your mind is dyed by your thoughts. Color your mind therefore with a succession of thoughts like these, for example: Where it is possible to live, it is also possible to live the good life; it is possible to live in a palace, therefore it is also possible to live the good life in a palace. Or again: each thing is made with that in view for the sake of which it was made; it is drawn towards that for which it was made; its end is found in that to which it is drawn; and where its end is, there too the advantage and the good of each is to be found. Now the good of a rational creature lies in a community, and it has long ago been shown that we are born for association in a community. For surely it is clear that the inferior exist for the sake of the better, and the better for the sake of each other. Now what is endowed with life is better than what is lifeless, and what is endowed with Reason is better than the merely alive.

17. To pursue what is impossible is madness; it is impossible that inferior men should not perform actions which are inferior.

18. Nothing happens to any man which he was not born

able to endure. What happened to you happened also to another, and he, through either ignorance that it happened or a desire to display high-mindedness, remains undisturbed and unharmed. Is it not terrible that ignorance and the desire to impress are stronger than wisdom?

19. Things cannot in themselves touch the soul at all; they have no entrance to it, cannot deflect or move it; it is the soul alone which deflects or moves itself, and it fashions external events to depend upon the judgment which it deems itself worthy to make about them.

20. In one way man is very close to us, insofar as we must do good to him and tolerate him, but insofar as some men stand in the way of my proper duties, man is among things indifferent to me, no less than the sun, the wind or a wild beast. These can hinder some action, but they can be no obstacle to our desire or our state of mind because of our power of remaining uncommitted and of adaptation.[5] The mind adapts any obstacle and turns it into a means toward its preferred aim, so that what hinders a particular action becomes a means to action, and an obstacle on a particular path becomes a help.

21. Honor that which is the best of all things in the universe; it makes use of all and governs all. Similarly, of things within you, honor that which is the best, and it is that which is akin to that other, for in your case too it is that which uses all else, and your life is directed by it.[6]

22. What brings no harm to the community does not harm its members. Whenever you think you have been injured, apply this rule: if the community is not hurt by it, then neither have I been hurt. If, on the other hand, the community has

[5] The wise man will start upon any course of action conditionally, i.e., he is prepared to find obstacles which make his original intention impossible to achieve; he can then adapt himself to the new situation and make that but another occasion for the practice of virtue. What really matters, and the only thing that does matter, is his state of mind. See Introd., p. xiii.

[6] The best thing in the universe is the universal Reason, the best in yourself is your own Reason which is a part of it.

been hurt, you should not be angry, but point out to him who hurt it what he has overlooked.

23. Reflect frequently on the swiftness with which things that are, or come to be, flow past and are carried away, for existence is like a river in perpetual flow; activities change continually; causes vary in innumerable ways; even that which is close to you hardly endures at all. The infinity of past and future time is a chasm in which all things vanish. Surely it is foolish for a man to be puffed up in the midst of this, to be excited or distressed as if his surroundings endured or his troubles were lasting.

24. Think of existence as a whole, in which you have a very small share; think of eternity, of which a brief and momentary portion has been allotted to you; think of destiny and how small a part of it is yours.

25. Another man does wrong. What is that to me? He will see to it; he has his own state of mind, his own activity. I possess now what the common nature of the universe wishes me to possess, and I perform such actions as my own nature wills me to perform.

26. Your directing mind, the ruler of your soul, must remain unaffected by the activity of your flesh, whether painful or pleasurable. It must not mingle with it but stay within its own frontiers and confine the affections of the body to their own sphere. When, however, these affections reach the mind through the other channel of common feeling, since both exist in a body organically one, then we should not resist this perception of them, since it is natural; but the directing mind should not add to this any judgment of its own as to whether the bodily affections are good or bad.[7]

27. Dwell with the gods. He dwells with the gods who at all times exhibits to them a soul satisfied with its apportioned

[7] The mind, that is, must not allow its judgment to be affected by bodily activities; though it will inevitably be conscious of bodily wants and the like, it must not be submerged by them or allow itself to be concerned with them.

lot, a soul which in its actions follows the command of the inner spirit, that fragment of himself which Zeus has given to every man as a champion and guide. And this is the intelligence and reason of every man.

28. Why be angry with a man because of his body odors or bad breath? What would you have him do? He has that kind of mouth, that kind of armpits, and they necessarily emit such odors. "But man is a rational being, and if he applies himself, he can understand what is wrong with him." Good for you! Then surely you too are rational, so stir up his reason with your own, inform him, put him in mind of it. If he listens to you, you will cure him, and there is no need of anger. You are neither a tragedian nor a whore.[8]

29. As you intend to live when you are gone, so you can live here and now. If the fates do not allow you so to live, then depart this life, but as one who suffers no ill. "The room is smoky and I leave it."[9] Why do you think that troublesome? But as long as no such reason drives me away, I remain here as a free man, and no one will prevent me doing what I wish, and I wish to do what is in accord with the nature of a rational and social being.

30. The intelligence of the Whole has the common good in view. Therefore it has fashioned the inferior for the sake of the higher, and brought the higher into harmony with each other. You see how it has put some below, others beside one another, and given each his due, and brought the ruling ones together to be of one mind.

31. How have you behaved until now toward the gods,

---

[8] This sentence has naturally puzzled commentators as to both meaning and connection with what precedes. Perhaps Marcus means that such weaknesses are nothing to you, you are not a dramatist (or actor) who has to represent the weaknesses of his fellow men, nor a whore who might well be brought into close physical contact with the offender.

[9] Marcus is not quoting exactly, but he clearly has in mind a passage of Epictetus (I. 25. 18): "Someone has caused smoke in the house; if it is a moderate amount, I shall stay; if it is too much, I shall leave. For remember and hold on to this: the door is open."

toward your parents, brother, wife, children, teachers, tutors, friends, relations, and slaves? Have you until now followed in relation to them all the old saying: "To do no evil and speak no evil"? [10] Remind yourself of what you have gone through, of what you have been able to endure; that the story of your life is already told and your days of service at an end; how often you have seen things of beauty, disregarded both pleasures and pains, foregone fame, and been kind to the foolish.

32. Why do unskilled and ignorant souls confound him who has both skill and knowledge? But what do you say is a skillful and knowing soul? One which knows the first principle and the end, and the Reason which permeates all existence and governs the Whole through all time in appointed cycles.

33. We shall very soon be only ashes or dry bones, merely a name or not even a name, while a name in any case is only a noise and an echo. The things much honored in life are vain, corruptible, and of no import. The living are like puppies who bite, or quarrelsome children who laugh and then immediately weep. Faith and Reverence and Justice and Truth "have left the wide-pathed earth for Heaven." [11] What is it which holds us here, if indeed the objects of sense are ever changing and last not, the senses themselves are blurred and variable as wax, our soul is but an exhalation from the blood, and good repute among such is vain? What holds us? To await death with good grace, whether it be extinction or a going elsewhere. And until the time for it comes, what suffices? What else but to honor the gods and praise them, to do good to men, bear with them and forbear. As for all that lies within the limits of mere flesh and mere life, remember that none of it belongs to you or is within your power.

34. Your life can always flow evenly if you can travel along the right road, if you understand and act with method. These

[10] The reference is to *Odyssey* IV. 690, where Penelope says of Odysseus that he never said or did anything unlawful, which is the right of kings.

[11] The reference is to a well-known and often imitated passage of Hesiod (*Works and Days*, 197-201) picturing Aidos (Reverence) and Nemesis abandoning the earth and returning to Olympus.

two things are common to the soul of a god and that of a man, indeed to that of any rational being: not to be hindered by another, and to achieve the good both in just disposition and just action, thus putting a limit to desire.

35. If this is no vice of mine, and is not due to any vice of mine, and the common good is not injured, then why am I disturbed about it? And what injury is there to the common good?

36. Do not be entirely swept along by the thought of another's grief. Help him as far as you can and as the case deserves, even if he is overwhelmed by the loss of indifferent things. Do not, however, imagine that he is suffering a real injury, for to develop that habit is a vice. Rather be like the old man who went off to beg for his foster child's top, fully aware that it was only a top; so must you do likewise. Well, then, when you are seen weeping on the rostrum, my good man, have you forgotten what these things are worth? [12] "Yes, but these men do long for them." Is that any reason for you also to be foolish?

37. "Once I was a lucky man whenever Fortune came upon me." To be lucky is to attribute good fortune to oneself, and good fortune means good dispositions of the soul, good impulses, good deeds.

[12] The reference is probably to the excitement and passionate language of an orator pleading his client's case or addressing a crowd in the forum. For the general thought of this section, cf. Epictetus, *Enchiridion* 16.

BOOK VI

1. The material substance of the Whole easily submits to persuasions and change. The Reason which governs it has within itself no motive for evil-doing, for it contains no evil. It does no wrong to anything, nor is anything injured by it, but all things come into being and run their course in accordance with it.

2. Let it be a matter of indifference whether you are cold or warm when doing what is fitting, whether you are nodding with sleep or have slept your fill, whether men speak ill or well of you, whether you are dying or doing something else. For death too is one of the actions of life, and we die as we perform it. Therefore, even when dying, it is sufficient that one's present task is well fulfilled.

3. Look within. Let not the proper quality of anything nor its value escape you.

4. All sensible things will very soon change, either to be taken into fire, if Being has been made one, or their atoms will be dispersed.[1]

5. The governing Reason knows its own condition, what it creates, and in what material.

6. The best method of defense is not to become like your enemy.

7. Find pleasure in this one thing and in it find repose: to proceed from one social action to another, remembering the god.

8. The directing mind is that which rouses itself, modifies itself, and makes itself such as it wishes to be, while making all that happens appear to itself such as it wishes it to be.

[1] That is, either the Stoic belief in the periodical conflagration which returns all things to divine fire, a world with purpose and Providence, or the Epicurean's world of atoms without purpose. Cf. IV. 3 and n. 2; also VI. 10.

9. All things are accomplished in accord with the nature of the Whole, for they cannot be in accord with any other nature, whether this be conceived as enveloping them, or contained within them, or external and separate.

10. Either a medley of entangled and dispersed atoms, or a unity of order and Providence. If the former, why am I eager to remain in such a haphazard concatenation and confusion? Why should I even care for anything but how to "return to earth"? Why be disturbed? The dispersal of atoms will come upon me whatever I do. If the latter, however, I worship and am content and derive courage from the governing Reason.

11. Whenever circumstances force disturbance upon you, return swiftly to yourself and do not be put out of step more than is inevitable. For you will be able to command harmony the better for continually making your way back to it.

12. If you had a stepmother and a mother at the same time, you would look after the former, but you would constantly return to the latter. This is what the palace and philosophy are to you. Frequently then return to, and find repose in, philosophy, which also makes the life of the palace bearable to you, and you bearable in it.

13. How useful, when roasted meats and other foods are before you, to see them in your mind as here the dead body of a fish, there the dead body of a bird or a pig. Or again, to think of Falernian wine as the juice of a cluster of grapes, of a purple robe as sheep's wool dyed with the blood of a shellfish, and of sexual intercourse as internal rubbing accompanied by a spasmodic ejection of mucus. What useful perceptual images these are! They go to the heart of things and pierce right through them, so that you see things for what they are. You must do this throughout life; when things appear too enticing, strip them naked, destroy the myth which makes them proud. For vanity is a dangerous perverter of Reason, and it is when you think your preoccupations most worthwhile that you are most enthralled. Look what Crates said even of Xenocrates.[2]

2 What Crates said is not known.

14. Most of the objects of popular admiration belong to the general class of things held together by coherence, such as stones and timber, or by a principle of natural growth such as figs, vines, or olives. The things admired by somewhat more temperate men belong to the class of things held together by a principle of life such as flocks, herds, or the simple owner-ship of a crowd of slaves. The things admired by men still more cultured are held together by rational soul, not, however, as rational but as endowed with craftsmanship or some other proficiency. But the man who prizes soul as rational and social is no longer involved with those other things at all, but above all else preserves his own soul's rational disposition and ac-tivity, and to this end co-operates with what is akin to himself.

15. Some things are hurrying to be born, others are hurrying to have been, and some part of that which is in process of being is already extinct. The streaming changes renew the universe continually, as the unceasing passage of time ever makes new the unending ages. What, among the things which rush past, can a man hold in high honor? It is as if one set out to love one of the sparrows flying past, and behold, it has vanished out of sight. Such indeed is life itself for every man, like an exhalation from the blood or a drawing breath from the air. As is the inhaling of air once and exhaling it again, which we do every moment, so too is the returning of the power of breathing as a whole, which you acquired at birth yesterday or the day before, to the source from which you drew it.

16. We should not greatly value the fact that we breathe through our pores, which plants do, or have a respiratory sys-tem like that of the animals, both tame and wild, or are im-pressed by sensual images, or are jerked this way and that like puppets on the strings of desire, or live in herds, or take nourishment, for this last is on a par with the ejection of food wastes. What then are we to value? Noisy applause? No, not even to be applauded by men's tongues, for the praise of the multitude is only a clacking of tongues. You have now also discarded that poor thing, fame. What is there left worthy of esteem? This, I think: to act or not to act in accordance with

the way we were made; to this all arts and crafts show the way, for it is the aim of every craft that its product be suited to the task for which it was made; it is also the aim of one who plants and nurses a vine, or tames horses, or trains dogs. What else is the concern of tutors and teachers?

Here then lies what is of value. If you are successful in this you will not esteem anything else as of much value for yourself. Will you then not cease to value many other things? Otherwise you will not be free, self-sufficient, or unperturbed, since the pursuit of those other things will compel you to feel envy and jealousy, to keep a watchful eye on those who have the power to deprive you of them, and to intrigue against those who possess what you esteem. In general, the man who needs any one of those things is inevitably in turmoil and utters many reproaches against the gods.

On the other hand, if you esteem and reverence the mind within you, you will be at peace with yourself, in tune with your fellows, and in harmony with the gods. You will, that is, be satisfied with whatever lot they have given you as your share, and prescribed for you.

17. Up, down and round about the elements are carried, but the activity of virtue does not reside in any of those motions; it is something more divine which goes forward on its successful journey, along a path hard to understand.

18. What strange conduct! They do not wish to speak well of men who live in their day and with them, yet they themselves attach much importance to the praise of a posterity which they have never seen and never will see. This is much the same as grieving because your ancestors did not speak in praise of you.

19. Do not, because something is hard for you to do, consider it impossible for man to achieve; but if anything is possible for man and his proper work, think that you too can achieve it.

20. Suppose that someone, in the course of our gymnastic training, has gashed us with his nails or struck us a butting

blow with his head; we do not make a case of it, or strike back, or suspect him in the future of intriguing against us. We do watch out for him, not as an enemy or with suspicion, but to swerve away from his blows without hostility. Something like this should happen in the other departments of life. We should overlook much in our opponents, for it is possible, as I said, to swerve away from blows without suspiciousness or hatred.

21. If someone can show me and prove to me that I am wrong in what I am thinking or doing, I shall gladly change it, for I seek the truth, which has never injured anyone. It is the man who persists in self-deception or ignorance who is injured.

22. I do my duty; other things do not disturb me, for they are either inanimate or irrational, or else they wander in ignorance of their road.

23. Deal with irrational creatures, with inanimate things generally, with objects of sense, proudly and freely, for you are endowed with reason while they are not; but your dealings with men, who have reason, must have a social aim. Invoke the gods' help in all things. And be not concerned with how long you may thus live, for three hours of such a life are sufficient.

24. Alexander the Great and his groom are reduced to the same state in death, for they have either been absorbed into the same creative Reason of the universe, or they have equally been scattered into atoms.

25. Reflect how many physical and mental processes take place at the same moment of time in each one of us; you will then not marvel that many more, or rather all things that come to be, are contained at the same moment in that over-all unity which we call the universe.

26. If anyone puts to you the question: How does one spell the name Antoninus?" will you get excited as you bring out each letter? And if they then lose their temper, will you lose yours too? Will you not gently proceed to enumerate each of the letters? So in your life here, remember that every duty is a sum of particular actions. These you must observe unper-

turbed, and complete the task at hand methodically without being yourself resentful of the resentment of others.

27. How cruel to prevent men from reaching out for things which they believe to be congenial and advantageous to them! And yet, in a way, you do not allow them to do this when you are angry because they do wrong, for they are surely drawn to what they think congenial and advantageous. "But it is not so." Well then, teach them and prove it to them, but without anger.

28. Death is a rest from the contradictions of sense perception, from being jerked like a puppet by the strings of desire, from the mind's analysis and the service of the flesh.

29. It is shameful in a life where the body does not fail you that the mind should fail you first.

30. See to it that you do not become Caesarized, or dyed with that coloring. For it does happen. Therefore treasure simplicity, goodness, purity, dignity, lack of affectation, love of justice, piety, kindliness, graciousness, and strength for your appropriate duties. Strive to remain such as philosophy wanted to make you. Revere the gods, protect men. Life is short. This earthly existence produces only one harvest: a godly disposition and social acts. Do all things as a disciple of Antoninus: imitate his keenness for logical action, his always equable temper, his piety, the serenity of his features, his sweetness, his lack of vainglory, his ambition to understand affairs. He dismissed no course of action till he had fully examined and clearly grasped it. He endured those who unjustly blamed him without blaming them in return. He never rushed things. He did not listen to slander. He was an exact judge of character and actions, but he was not given to reproaches, not afraid of rumors, not suspicious, no sophist. He was satisfied with little in the way of a house, of bedcovers, of clothes, food, and servants. He was fond of work and energetic, able to remain at the same task till evening without even needing to relieve himself except at his usual hour, because of his scanty diet. His friendships were constant and unchanging. He tolerated outspoken

opposition to his ideas and was glad if anyone showed him a better way. He was religious but free from superstition. Be his disciple in all this, and may your last hour find you as much at ease with your conscience as he was with his.

31. Sober yourself, summon yourself, awaken once more and, realizing that you were troubled by dreams, examine these realities as you then examined those dreams.[3]

32. I am made of body and soul. To the body all things are indifferent, for it cannot feel concern. To the mind all is indifferent except its own activities, and all its own activities are within its control. And of these it is concerned only with the present, for its future and past activities are themselves indifferent here and now.

33. Painful labor is not contrary to nature for the foot or the hand, as long as the foot fulfills the functions of a foot and the hand the functions of a hand. In the same way, painful labor is not contrary to the nature of man as man, as long as he fulfills the function of a man. And if it is not contrary to his nature, it is not an evil for him.

34. What pleasures have been enjoyed by pirates, catamites, parricides and tyrants! [4]

35. Do you not see how lowly craftsmen, though they accommodate the layman up to a point, nonetheless cling to the rational principle of their art and tolerate no departure from it? Is it not dreadful that an architect and a physician will respect the rational principle of their own particular craft more than a man respects his own rational principle, which he has in common with the gods?

36. Asia, Europe are corners of the universe. The whole ocean, a drop in the universe. Mount Athos, a clod of the uni-

[3] That is, just as when you wake you realize that you were troubled only by dreams, you should now realize that the so-called realities of life, and the anxieties which they cause, are as dreams compared to true reality.

[4] And therefore such pleasures are of no value and among indifferent things.

verse. The whole of our present age is a point in eternity. All things are small, changeable, vanishing.

All things come thence, either originating in the common directing mind, or as incidental consequences. The maw of the lion, poison, every kind of evil deed, are, like thorns or mud, but incidental accretions on things noble and lovely. Do not think of them as alien to that which you worship, but concentrate your thoughts on the source of all things.

37. He who has seen the present has seen everything, all that from eternity has come to pass, and all that will come to be in infinite time. For everything is akin and the same.

38. Reflect frequently how all things in the universe are linked to one another and how they are related. For in a sense all things are interwoven and therefore in friendly sympathy. All things follow one another because of the active tension and the common spirit breathing through them all, and because of the unity of all existence.

39. Adapt yourself to the things which have been allotted to you, and love those whom you have drawn as your associates, with true love.

40. Every instrument, tool and utensil is satisfactory if it fulfills the task for which it was fashioned, though he who fashioned it is an outside agent. But in the case of things organically held together by nature, the power which fashioned them is within. You must therefore reverence it more, and believe that if your disposition and conduct through life are in accordance with its purpose, all is satisfactory to your intelligence. And so with the Whole, the things within it satisfy its intelligence.

41. Whenever you imagine something outside your control to be good or evil, you must inevitably blame the gods for the presence of such evil or the absence of such good, and you will hate men as the real or suspected cause of both. We commit many wrongs through our concern for such things. But if we judge to be good or evil only those things which are within

our power, we have no reason left either to blame a god or to face a man as his enemy.

42. We all work together to one end, some of us with conscious understanding, others without knowing it, as Heraclitus, I believe, says that even those who sleep are at work producing together what comes to be in the universe.[5] Each makes a different contribution, and even one who objects and tries to oppose and destroy what comes to be, contributes beyond his intention, for the universe needed even him. For the rest, decide on which side you will take your place. For the Reason which governs all will in any case make good use of you and admit you to a place among its fellow workers and co-operators, but do not you become as trivial and ridiculous a part of them as the line in the play mentioned by Chrysippus.[6]

43. Does the sun-god deem it right to do the work of the god of rain, or Asclepius that of the goddess of harvest? What of each of the stars? Are they not different, yet co-operate to the same end?

44. If the gods made plans for me and for what should happen to me, they made the right plans, for it is not easy even to conceive of a god counseling ill; and what reason had they to want to harm me? How could this be of benefit to them or to the common good on whose behalf above all they exercise their providence? If they did not make plans for me in particular, yet they certainly planned the general good, and as incidental consequences of this I should love and welcome what happens to me. If they do not plan at all—this it is impious to believe, or else let us not sacrifice or pray to them, not swear by them or do any of those other acts which we perform on the assumption that the gods are present and live alongside of us. But if they do not make plans for any one of us in particular, yet I may plan for myself and examine my own ad-

[5] Heraclitus, fr. 75 (Diels).

[6] What Chrysippus said is preserved by Plutarch (*Against the Stoics* 1065d). It was to the effect that certain lines of comedy, in themselves poor, yet contribute to the charm of the play when seen in their context.

vantage. And the advantage of each is what is in accord with his own make-up and his own nature, for my nature is rational and social.

My city and my country, as I am Antoninus, is Rome; as I am a man, it is the world. Therefore, only the things which are beneficial to these communities are good for me.

45. Whatever happens to an individual is beneficial to the Whole. To know this was sufficient. However, if you observe carefully, you will generally also see that whatever benefits one man also benefits other men; but in this context the word "benefit," applying as it does to indifferent things, is to be taken in its more generally accepted sense.

46. As the performances in the amphitheater bore you because you are always seeing the same things and the monotony makes the spectacle tiresome, so too you feel about the whole of life: everything up and down is the same and due to the same causes. How much longer then?

47. Reflect continually that death has come to all sorts of men of all sorts of occupations and all sorts of communities, right down to Philistion, Phoebus, and Origanion.[7] Turn now to other races, and the same is true. We must then change our abode to where so many clever orators have gone, so many worthy philosophers like Heraclitus, Pythagoras, and Socrates, so many earlier heroes and later generals and despots, and besides these Eudoxus, Hipparchus, and Archimedes. Many other men of quick mind or high intelligence have gone there, men who worked hard, men who were knavish or willful, and even those who mocked at the fated briefness of human life itself, as Menippus did and others like him. Reflect about all these, that they have long been dead. This is nothing dreadful for them, and why should it be so for those who have made no name at all for themselves? There is in this life only one thing of much value, to live with truth and righteousness, and to be kind to liars and sinners.

[7] These three names presumably refer to contemporaries, perhaps members of Marcus' household, but we are not sure.

48. When you want to rejoice, think of the good qualities of your associates: the energy of one, the spirit of reverence in another, the liberality of a third, some other quality in a fourth. For nothing gives as much joy as to observe manifestations of virtue in the character of one's associates, the more of them at once, the better. So keep them before your eyes.

49. Are you resentful because you weigh only so many pounds and not over two hundred? No more should you resent that you have only so many years to live and no more. Just as you are satisfied with the amount of matter allotted to your make-up, so you should be satisfied with your allotment of years.

50. Try to persuade them, and do so even against their will, whenever the rational principle of justice leads you to do so. But if someone prevents you by force, change your course and aim to feel content and unhurt, thus making use of the obstacle to attain another virtue. Remember that you set out on the first course conditionally, and that you did not aim at achieving the impossible. What was your aim then? Some such impulse as led you to pursue your first objective, and in this you succeed, and the inner conditions which led us to the first course have been realized.

51. The lover of glory finds his own good in the actions of another, the lover of pleasure finds it in a passive state of his own; the wise man finds it in his own actions.[8]

52. It is possible to form no opinion of this and not to be distressed in mind, for the nature of things is not such as to create our judgments about them.

53. Accustom yourself not to be inattentive to what another person says, and as far as possible enter into his mind.

[8] The lover of glory is obviously dependent upon the esteem in which others hold him, the honor they pay him, etc.; physical pleasures depend very largely upon external stimulants and circumstances which are not within one's control; the Stoic wise man, whose whole happiness depends on himself, his own state of mind and doing his duty, is not dependent on anyone.

54. That which does not benefit the swarm does not benefit the bee.

55. If sailors spoke ill of their navigator or the sick of their doctor, would they pay attention to anything else except how he would bring about the safety of the passengers or the health of the patients?[9]

56. How many with whom I entered the world have already gone.

57. Jaundice makes honey seem bitter, a mad dog's' bite makes one fear water, and small boys believe a little round ball to be a thing of beauty. Why should I be angry with them? And do you not think that untrue notions have as much power over men as bile has over the jaundiced or poison over the victim of hydrophobia?

58. No one will prevent you from living in accordance with the rationality of your own nature. Nothing will happen to you which is contrary to the rationality of the common nature of the world.

59. What kind of men they wish to please! By what means and by what deeds do they succeed? How soon time will hide everything; how many things it has already hidden.

[9] Marcus seems to have in mind that he should be judged by others entirely in his capacity as ruler, but that men say many things about him which have nothing to do with this.

BOOK VII

1. What is wickedness? It is this which you have often seen. Whatever occurs, be ready with the thought that it is what you have often seen. You will generally find the same things everywhere: the histories of ancient, middle or modern times are full of them; our cities and homes are full of them now. Nothing is new; everything is familiar and lasts but a little while.

2. Your doctrines live. How else do they become dead except when the mind's images which correspond to them are extinguished; and to rekindle these constantly into life is within your power. I can understand what I ought about this event. If I can do so, then why am I perturbed? What lies outside my mind is of no concern to it. Learn this and stand upright. You can live anew. Look upon things as you used to look upon them, for to do so is to live anew.[1]

3. The empty pursuit of triumphal parades, the dramas of the stage, flocks and herds, battles with the spear, a bone thrown to puppies, scraps thrown into fish tanks, the calamities and burdens of ants, the scurryings of excited mice, puppets jerked by strings—amidst these you must stand with kindliness and without insolence, but realizing that the worth of each depends upon the worth of his pursuits.

4. When things are being said, one should follow every word, when things are being done, every impulse; in the latter

---

[1] Images in the mind, φαντασίαι, are of many kinds, good or bad, and they motivate actions. They are good if they are under the control of the directing mind, in accordance with the right principles, and lead to the right kind of actions; they are bad when they reflect passions and unnecessary desires, and thus lead to the satisfaction of those passions and desires. Marcus means that the continual application of right principles to action, by way of the right mental images, keeps those principles and doctrines alive.

case, to see straightway to what object the impulse is directed, in the former, to watch closely what meaning is expressed.[2]

5. Is my mind able to cope with this? If it is, then I use it for this task like a tool provided for me by the nature of the Whole; if my mind cannot cope with it, either I yield the task to someone better qualified to complete it, unless it is for other reasons my duty,[3] or I perform it as best I can and call in to assist me someone who can with the help of my directing mind do what is opportune and useful to the community. For whatever I do, whether by myself or with the assistance of another, must be directed only to what is socially useful and fitting.

6. All those who were famous of old have been surrendered to oblivion, and all those who sang their fame have vanished long ago.

7. Do not feel shame at being helped. It is your purpose to perform the task before you, as a soldier does in a siege. What if you, being lame, cannot reach the battlements alone but can do so with another's assistance?

8. Be not disturbed by the future. You will come to it, if you must, endowed with the same Reason with which you face the present.

9. All things are interwoven with one another, and the bond which unites them is sacred; practically nothing is alien to anything else, for all things are combined with one another and contribute to the order of the same universe. The universe embraces all things and is one, and the god who pervades all

---

2 Marcus probably means that one should understand the motives of other people's actions and their real meaning, that this understanding will prevent anger and resentment; but as far as the Greek goes it might mean that one should understand the motivations of one's own actions and watch one's own words closely so as to express one's meaning clearly. Cf. VII. 30.

3 Reading, with the MSS, ἐὰν . . . μὴ καθήκῃ. The meaning then is that I yield unless the action is my duty; if it is I cannot leave it to another but must perform it myself as best I can and with what help I can secure. One imagines that the Emperor must often have faced tasks he did not feel very qualified to perform, but which he could not hand over to others.

things is one, the substance is one, the law is one, the Reason common to all thinking beings is one, the truth is one, if indeed there is one perfection for the kindred beings who share in this selfsame Reason.

10. All that is material very soon disappears in the universal substance; every cause is very soon taken up into the universal Reason, and the memory of each event is very soon absorbed into eternity.

11. For a creature endowed with reason, an action in accord with its nature is also in accord with reason.

12. Be upright or be put right.

13. Rational beings in their separate bodies are as closely related to each other as the limbs of one body; for they were created for co-operation in a common task. This thought will strike you more if you frequently say to yourself: "I am a limb of a composite whole consisting of rational beings." But if, changing the word,[4] you call yourself merely a part instead of a limb, you do not yet love your fellow men from the heart, nor derive complete joy from doing good; you will do it merely as a duty, not as doing good to yourself.

14. Let any external event happen to those who can be affected by it. Those affected can, if they wish, find fault with it; as for me, if I do not consider its happening to be an evil, I am not yet injured. And it lies with me not to consider it as such.

15. "Whatever anyone does or says, I must be good." This is as if gold or purple or an emerald were always saying: "Whatever anyone does or says, I must be an emerald and retain my own color."

16. The directing mind does not disturb itself, never, for example, frightens itself or lures itself into desire.[5] If anyone else can frighten or pain it, let him do so, for it will not itself

4 In the Greek it is the change of one letter only, the λ of μέλος (limb) to the ρ of μέρος (part).

5 The text is uncertain here. For the animal soul and the independence of the thinking and directing mind, compare II. 2 and n. 1.

turn its understanding into such paths. Let the body concern itself that it does not suffer, if it can; and if it does suffer, let it say so, but it is the animal soul which feels fear and pain. The part which understands these things does not suffer at all, for it will not hasten to judge that it does. In itself the directing mind is without needs unless it creates a need for itself, so too it is undisturbed and unhindered unless it disturbs and hinders itself.

17. Happiness is a blessed genius or a divine blessing.[6] Why then do you, my imagination, behave like this? Go away, by the gods, as you came, for I have no need of you. You came through force of ancient habit. I am not angry with you, only go away.

18. Does a man fear change? What can come to be without change? What is more dear or belongs more to the nature of the Whole? Can you yourself take a bath unless the furnace wood undergo change? Can you be fed, unless your nourishment suffer change? Can any other useful thing be done without change? Do you not see then that for you too to be changed is precisely similar, and similarly necessary to the universal nature?

19. All physical things journey through the universal substance as through a swollen torrent, by nature akin to, and cooperating with, the Whole, as our limbs do with one another. How many a Chrysippus, a Socrates, an Epictetus the ages have already swallowed. Let this thought be with you about any man or thing whatsoever.

20. I have only one anxiety: that I myself should do some-

6 Marcus is playing on the etymology of the word εὐδαιμονία, happiness, which is derived from εὖ (well) and δαίμων, which means a divine being, and is also used of the lot of a man personified, being then thought of as a familiar spirit or genius, who accompanied or directed man on his life's journey; the next two words are uncertain. I have adopted Farquharson's reading δαιμόνιον ἀγαθόν, taking the former as an adjective.

The imaginings which are told to go away in what follows are presumably the bad φαντασίαι (see VII. 2 and n. 1).

thing which our human constitution does not want done, or done in this way or at this time.

21. You will soon forget everything. Everything will soon forget you.

22. It is human to love even those who falter, and you will do so if you reflect that people are akin, that they do wrong through ignorance and unwillingly, that you will both be dead in a little while, and, above all, that he has done you no injury, for he did not make your directing mind worse than it was before.

23. The nature of the Whole fashioned from the whole substance, as from wax, at one time a horse, then dissolved it and used its matter to make a tree, then a man, then something else, and each of these lasts but a very short time. There is nothing fearful for a box in dissolution, any more than in its being made.

24. An excessively angry look is contrary to nature, and, if it is frequent, grace of feature dies out or is extinguished in the end so that it cannot be rekindled at all.[7] Try to understand from this that it is against reason. For if even awareness of one's wrongdoing disappears, what reason is there left to live?

25. All the things which you see will very soon be changed by the nature which governs the Whole; it will make other things from their substance, and then other things again from the substance of these, in order that the universe may always preserve its youth and vigor.

26. Whenever anyone wrongs you, consider what view of good or evil prompted his action. Realizing this, you will pity him, be neither surprised nor angry at him. For either you yourself have the same view of good as he, or one like it, and then you must forgive him; if, on the other hand, you no longer view good and evil in this way, you will the more easily feel kindly to one who sees things awry.

[7] The text is hopelessly corrupt and the meaning can only be conjectural.

27. Do not daydream that you possess what you do not; but take thought for the most fortunate things which are yours, and call to mind on their account how they would be missed if you did not have them. Be also careful, however, that your joy in them does not lead you to overestimate them and to be perturbed by their occasional absence.

28. Gather yourself within yourself. Your directing mind is by nature self-sufficient, if you act rightly and are at peace for that very reason.

29. Erase imaginings. Still the puppet-strings of passion. Circumscribe the present. Recognize what is happening to you or to another. Analyze and divide any event into its cause and its matter; think of your last hour; leave the wrong done by another at the place where it was done.

30. Give your full attention to what is said. Apply your mind to what is being done and to who does it.

31. Find joy in simplicity, self-respect, and indifference to what lies between virtue and vice. Love the human race. Follow the divine. It was said that "all things exist by convention, only the elements are real." Suffice it to remember "all is convention." [8] This is little enough.

32. About death: either a scattering, if we are atoms; or, if all is one, either extinction or change of place.

33. About pain: that which is unendurable carries us off; that which lasts can be endured.[9] The mind preserves its own calm by withdrawal. The directing mind has not been made worse; as for the parts injured by pain, let any such part prove it, if it can.

34. About fame: look at their thoughts, of what kind they are, what kind of things they avoid or pursue; and as drifting sand hides the sand that was there before, so in life the earlier is very soon hidden by what comes after.

[8] The reference seems to be to a statement attributed to Democritus by Diogenes Laertius (IX. 72) to the effect that qualities such as hot and cold exist only by convention ($\nu\acute{o}\mu\psi$) and atoms are the only reality.

[9] Based on a saying of Epicurus (Plutarch, De Audiendis Poetis 36b).

35. Do you think that a mind of great nobility which contemplates all time and all existence will consider human life to be a matter of great importance? Impossible, said he. And will he think death a terrible thing? Not in the least.[10]

36. A king's privilege: to do good and be ill spoken of.[11]

37. It is shameful for the countenance to be obedient, to be shaped and ordered at the bidding of the mind while the mind fails to shape and order itself.

38. Useless to vent one's anger on mere things, since they cannot care.[12]

39. May you give joy both to the gods and us.

40. To harvest life like a full ear of corn. This man to be, the other not to be.

41. If gods neglect both me and my two sons, this too has reason to it.

42. The good is on my side, and so is justice.

43. Join not in lamentation, nor in wild excitement.

44. I should be right to answer him: "You are wrong, my friend, if you think that a man of even small worth should take into account the risk of life and death, and not look to this only when he acts, whether his actions are right or wrong, whether he acts like a good or a bad man." [13]

45. For this, gentlemen, is the truth: Whatever post a man has himself taken up, thinking it to be best, or has been ordered to take up by his commander, there he must, I think, remain and face danger, without a thought for death or for anything else but the shame of flight.

46. But consider, my good sir, whether nobility and goodness are not something very different from saving one's life or having it saved. A true man should dismiss the question

10 From Plato, *Republic* VI. 486a-b.

11 This is said to be from Antisthenes (Epictetus IV. 6. 20).

12 The quotations in 38 and 40-43 are from lost plays of Euripides. That in 39 has not been traced.

13 The quotations in this and the next section are from Plato's *Apology* 28b, and that in section 46 from his *Gorgias* 512d-e.

of how long his life lasts; he must not be in love with mere life, but leave these things to the gods and, believing what women say—namely that no one can escape his fate—he must consider how he can best live his allotted span.

47. Observe the courses of the stars as if you were to run those courses with them; have constantly in mind the changes of the elements into one another, for such thoughts sweep away the squalor of life on earth.

48. And when you talk about men you should look upon things on earth as one who looks from above on things below: flocks, military camps, farms, marriages, divorces, births, deaths, the noisy confusion of the courts, desolate places, varied foreign races, feasts, lamentations, market places, the whole medley and order derived from opposites.

49. Look back upon the past: so many changes of rulers. One can also foresee the future, for it will be altogether similar and cannot deviate from the rhythm of the present. Hence to examine human life for forty years is the same as to examine it for ten thousand years, for what more will you see?

50. Also:

> Things sprung from earth to earth returned,
> And those that grew from birth in heaven
> Found a way back to the deep sky.[14]

Or this: dispersal of the interwoven atoms and scattering of the unfeeling elements.

51. Also:

> Those who, with food or drink or magic arts
> Divert the stream, so that they may not die.

> Whatever wind blows from the gods on high
> We must endure, and labor without tears.

52. "A better wrestler," [15] but not more socially minded or

---

[14] Another fragment of Euripides, as is the first quotation in section 51. The next two lines are of unknown origin.

[15] Plutarch (*Apophth. Spart.* 236e) tells this story. A young Spartan had been defeated at Olympia (presumably in a wrestling match). Men said "Your opponent is a better (κρείττων) man than you." "No," he replied, "he is a better wrestler."

more respectful or more disciplined to accept his fate, or more kindly to his erring neighbors.

53. Where a task can be completed in accordance with Reason, which gods and men have in common, there is nothing to fear; where one can be benefited by an activity which proceeds on its satisfactory way in accordance with our human constitution, no injury should be anticipated.

54. Everywhere and at all times it is within your power to show reverence towards the gods by being satisfied with your lot, to deal justly with those you meet along your way, and to pay loving attention to the impressions present in your mind, so that nothing you have not grasped can invade it unperceived.

55. Do not divert your attention to the directing minds of others; look straight ahead to where Nature is leading you, to the nature of the Whole through what befalls you, and your own nature through what you must do, for every man must do what is compatible with his own make-up. For the other parts of man have been constituted for the sake of his rational parts, just as in the world at large the lower exists for the sake of the higher, but rational creatures exist for each other's sake. Now the first principle of the human make-up is social obligation, the second is resistance to the persuasions of the flesh, for it is characteristic of the activity of reason and the intellect to set itself apart and never to be overcome by the activities of sense-perception and of desire. Both of these are like animals, whereas the activity of the intellect wants to be pre-eminent and never to be overcome by the others. And rightly so, for it naturally uses all the others. The third principle in the make-up of a being endowed with reason is to be free from haste and deceit. Let the directing mind cling to these principles and keep to the straight road ahead; it will then fulfill its own function.

56. As if you had already died and lived only till now, live the rest of your life as a kind of bonus, in accord with nature.

57. Only love your present lot and fate, for what could be more suited to you?

58. In every contingency have before your eyes those to whom the same thing happened before. They were vexed, astonished, reproachful. Where are they now? Nowhere. Well then, do you wish to act as they did? Why not leave the ways of others to those who act in accordance to them and conform to them, and be yourself wholly concerned with how to make use of these contingencies? You will then make good use of them and they will be to you the raw material of life. Only pay attention, and desire every one of your actions to be right in your own judgment, and remember two things: your actions are significant, but the circumstances in which they take place have no significance.

59. Dig down within yourself, where the source of goodness is ever ready to gush forth, if you always dig deeply.

60. The body too must be made steady; neither its activity nor its attitude should toss it about. Just as the mind watches over the face and enables it to express wisdom and grace, so the whole body should acquire similar control. And all this should be achieved without making it a primary aim.

61. The art of living is more like wrestling than dancing, insofar as one should stand ready for, and not be thrown by, whatever happens unexpectedly.

62. Keep constantly in mind who these men are whom you want to testify in your favor, and what kind of directing minds they have. You will not then reproach those who err involuntarily, and you will not need their testimony, if you look at the sources of their assumptions and desires.

63. "Every soul," he says, "is unwilling to be deprived of the truth" [16]—or to be deprived of justice, of moderation, of kindliness, of every such virtue. It is very necessary constantly to remember this, for it will make you more gentle toward all men.

64. Whenever you suffer pain, have the thought ready that

[16] From Epictetus (I. 28. 4), who attributes the saying to Plato. The thought is thoroughly Platonic (e.g., *Rep*. III. 413a) but the exact words do not occur in Plato.

there is no shame attached to it and that it does no harm to the directing mind since it does not harm the latter in its reasoning or social aspects. Let the saying of Epicurus help you in most cases: "Pain is neither unendurable nor everlasting, if you remember its limitations and do not add to it in thought."[17] Remember also that there are many distressing things which are identical with pain without our realizing it—sleepiness, for example, and fever, and lack of appetite. Whenever you are distressed by one of these, say to yourself that you are yielding to pain.

65. Take care that you do not have toward the inhuman the same feelings as they have toward mankind.

66. How do we know that Telauges was not a better person than Socrates? It is not enough that Socrates died more gloriously, that he disputed more skillfully with the Sophists, that he showed more hardihood in spending a whole night outside in freezing weather, that, when ordered to bring in the man from Salamis he thought it nobler to refuse, and that he "swaggered in the streets," about which last one might well wonder if it was true.[18] What we need to examine is the nature of Socrates' soul, whether he could find satisfaction in being just toward men and pious toward the gods, in not being heedlessly angry with vice or subservient to anyone's ignorance, whether he accepted any part of the fate allotted to him from the Whole as alien to himself and bore it as an intolerable burden, whether he allowed his intelligence to share the suffering of his paltry flesh.

67. Nature has not so blended you into the whole mixture as not to allow you to keep yourself separate and to keep what is your own within your own power. Remember that always, and also this: to live in happiness depends on very few things. Do not think that, because you despaired of being a logician

---

[17] This saying of Epicurus is not found in our texts, but see VII. 33 and n. 9 above.

[18] For these stories about Socrates see Plato, *Symposium* 220b-d, *Apology* 32c-d: and Aristophanes, *Clouds* 362-63.

or a natural scientist, you therefore despair of being free, self-respecting, socially minded and obedient to the divine. It is altogether possible for a man to be godlike and not to be recognized as such by anyone.

68. Live your life free from compulsion in utmost gladness of heart, even if all men shout against you whatever they will, even if wild beasts tear limb from limb this doughlike matter which has grown around you. What in all this prevents the mind from keeping its own peace, its own capacity for true judgment of the surrounding circumstances, and its readiness to make use of present contingencies, so that the judgment says to circumstance: "This is what you really are, though to common opinion you appear different," and readiness to use says to contingency: "I was looking for you, for I always consider the present to be the raw material for rational and social virtue, and, in general terms, for the art of man or god." Indeed a man or a god can make whatever happens his own; it is neither new to him nor hard to deal with, but familiar and easy to work on.

69. This is proper to a perfect character: to spend each day as if it were one's last, without excitement, torpor, or pretense.

70. The gods, who are immortal, are not vexed that through such a length of time they must always endure so many and such inferior creatures; moreover, they care for them in all sorts of ways. Do you then, who are almost on the point of death, refuse to do so, even though you are one of the inferior creatures yourself?

71. It is ridiculous not to escape from one's own vices, which it is possible to do, but to flee from the vices of others, which is impossible.

72. Whatever the rational or social capacity finds to be neither intelligent nor socially useful, it judges to be inferior to itself, with good reason.

73. Whenever you have done a good deed, and another has been benefited, why do you, as fools do, look for a third thing

beyond these, be it a reputation for doing good, or getting something in return.

74. No one wearies of receiving benefits, and to benefit others is to act in accord with nature. Do not then weary of deriving benefit from benefiting others.

75. The nature of the Whole had an impulse to create the universe; now either all that comes to birth arises as a consequence of this, or even the most important ends, toward which the ruling mind of the universe directs its own impulse, are irrational. Remembering this will make you face many things more calmly.

BOOK VIII

1. This too contributes to dispelling vainglory, that you are no longer free to have spent your whole life, or your adult life at least, as a philosopher, but it is clear to many, as it is to yourself, that you are far from philosophy. You live in confusion, so that it is no longer easy for you to attain a philosophic reputation, for your station in life is against it. If then you realize the situation truly, abandon thoughts of future reputation and be satisfied to live whatever remains of life as your nature demands. Observe what it does demand, and let nothing else distract you. You know from experience in how many directions you have wandered, and that you did not find the good life anywhere, not in reasoning, not in wealth, not in reputation, not in pleasures—nowhere. Where then is the good life to be found? In doing what the nature of man requires. And how is one to do this? By holding fast to doctrines that direct one's desires and actions. What doctrines? Those concerning good and evil: that nothing is good for a man which does not make him just, temperate, brave, and free; nothing evil which does not make him the opposite of these.

2. Ask yourself this about your every action: "How does this affect me? Shall I feel remorse about it?" Death is very near and then all will be gone. What more do I require, if this is the action of an intelligent and social creature, one who lives under the same law as the divine.

3. Alexander, Caesar, Pompey—what are they compared with Diogenes, Heraclitus, Socrates? The latter men saw the nature of things, its causes and its substances, and their directing minds were their own, while the former had to care for so many things and were enslaved to so many ends.

4. They will go on doing the same things no less even if you burst yourself with anger.

5. First, be unperturbed, for all things are in accord with the nature of the Whole, and in a short while you will not be anyone, anywhere—as neither Hadrian nor Augustus is now. Then, further, pay attention to the matter in hand, observe it in itself; remember that you need to be a good man and what the nature of man requires. Do this without turning back, and say what seems to you most just. Only act with kindness, reverence and sincerity.

6. The task of the universal nature is to transfer things from one place to another, to change them, to lift them hence and take them yonder. All things are in process of change, so that novelty should not cause fear; all things are akin, and their distribution is, moreover, equalized.[1]

7. Every nature is satisfied when it travels the right road, and a nature endowed with reason travels the right road if, in its imaginings, it does not assent to what is false or what is obscure, if it directs its impulses on the straight path which leads only to social actions, if it limits its desires and aversions to what is within our power, and welcomes whatever is allotted to it by the common nature. For it is a part of this universal nature as the nature of the leaf is part of the nature of the plant, except that in that case the leaf's nature is part of a nature which possesses neither perception nor reason, and can be hindered by externals. But the nature of man is part of a nature unhindered, intelligent and just, if indeed it grants to each creature its equal and deserved share of time, substance, cause, activity and circumstance. Consider then, not whether you will find a one-to-one correspondence in the endowments of each, but whether, taken as a whole, all that is given to one is equal to the total endowments of the other.

8. Impossible to read. But it is possible to refrain from arrogance, it is possible to conquer pleasure and pain, to be above vainglory; it is possible not to be angry with the insensitive and the ungrateful, nay, even to care for them.

---

[1] I have kept the original order in this last sentence. Farquharson transposes the clause "so that novelty should not cause fear" to the end of the section.

9. Let no one, not even yourself, any longer hear you putting the blame on palace life.

10. To repent is to reproach oneself for having neglected to do something useful; what is good must, in a sense, be useful, and the good man must give heed to it; but no good man repents having neglected some pleasure. Pleasure is therefore neither good nor useful.

11. What is this in itself, in its own composition? What is its essence, its substance, its cause, what is its function in the world? How long does it persist?

12. When you wake from sleep with difficulty, remind yourself that it is in accord with your constitution and with your human nature to perform social acts, whereas sleep we share with irrational animals. And what is in accord with the nature of each is more congenial, more his own, and indeed more agreeable.

13. Continually, and, if possible, in the case of every mental image, consider its nature, realize its emotional content, and judge it rationally.

14. Whomsoever you meet, straightway say to yourself: What belief does this man hold about good and evil? For if he holds such and such beliefs about pleasure and pain and what produces them, about a good or evil reputation, about death and life, I shall not think it surprising or strange if his actions are such and such, and I shall remember that he is compelled to act in this manner.

15. Remember that, just as one would feel shame to be surprised if a fig tree bears figs, so one should be ashamed to feel surprised if the universe bears the particular produce of which there is a crop. And a doctor would be ashamed to be surprised if a patient developed a fever, or a pilot if a contrary wind arose.

16. Remember that to change your course and to obey one who sets you right are both equally characteristic of a free man. For the action is yours, in accord with your desire and judgment, in accord with your intelligence.

17. If it is within your power, why do you do it? If within the power of another, whom do you blame—atoms or gods? To do either is folly. No one is to blame. If you can, set him right; if you cannot do this, set the matter itself right. If you cannot do even this, then what further good will blaming bring you? And nothing should be done without purpose.

18. That which has died does not fall outside the universe. If it remains here and is changed, here too it is dissolved into its everlasting parts, which are the elements of the universe and yours. These are themselves changed and they do not grumble.

19. Everything came into being for a purpose, be it a horse, or a vine. Why does this surprise you? Even the Sun will say: "I was born for a purpose," and so will the other gods. For what purpose, then, were you born? For pleasure? Consider whether this idea can be maintained.

20. The cessation of each thing is no less the aim of nature than its birth or its duration. As when a man tosses a ball, in what way is it good for the ball to rise, or bad for it to drop, or even to have fallen on the ground? How is it good for a bubble to form and bad for it to burst? And the same can be said of the flame of a lamp.

21. Look at it from all sides and observe what kind of thing it is, what it becomes in old age, in illness, in debauch.

He who praises is a short-lived creature, so is the object of his praise, and so is he who remembers and he who is remembered. Moreover, not even in this your corner of your region of the earth do all men agree, nor is a man in agreement with himself. And the whole earth is only a point in space.

22. Pay attention to the object or the action before you, or the principle it embodies, or the meaning of words spoken about it.

What you endure is right: you would rather become good tomorrow than be good today.

23. When I act, I relate my action to the benefiting of man-

kind; when something happens to me I accept it and relate it to the gods and to the common source in which all events are interrelated.

24. Just as taking a bath seems to you a matter of oil, sweat, dirt, scummy water, all of it offensive, so is every part of life and every kind of matter.

25. Lucilla buried Verus, then Lucilla herself died.[2] So with Secunda and Maximus, Epitynchanus and Diotimus, Antoninus and Faustina. And so with all: Celer buried Hadrian, and then died. Those clever people, whether prudent or conceited, where are they? Charax, for example, and Demetrius and Eudaimon, who were certainly clever, and any other who was like them. All creatures of a day, all dead long since. Some not remembered even for a brief while, some turned into legends, and some by now vanished even from legend. Remember then that either the puny mixture of atoms, which is you, must be scattered, or your spirit must be extinguished or journey elsewhere and be assigned another post.

26. A man's joy is to do what is specifically human, and it is specifically human to be gracious to his kind, to despise the activities of the senses, to judge aright the persuasive pictures of the imagination, to contemplate the nature of the Whole and all that happens in accord with it.

27. Three attitudes: one to the circumstances which surround you, the second to the divine cause from which all things come to all men, the third to those around you.

28. Pain is either an evil for the body—then let the body prove it so—or for the soul. The soul, however, can preserve its own fair weather and calm, and not accept it as an evil. For every judgment, impulse, desire, and aversion is within the soul, and no evil can penetrate there.

[2] Lucilla is probably Domitia Lucilla, mother of Marcus, and Verus is then M. Annius Verus, her husband and Marcus' father. Secunda is probably the wife of Claudius Maximus, Marcus' friend and teacher. Faustina is the wife of Antoninus Pius and Marcus' aunt. Epitynchanus, Diotimus, Charax and Eudaimon are not known. Nor can we tell which Demetrius is referred to. It may be the Cynic philosopher banished by Vespasian.

29. Efface the impressions of your imagination by continually saying to yourself: "It now lies within my power that there be no vice or passion, no disturbance at all, in this my soul, but I see all things for what they are and deal with them on their merits." Remember that the capacity to do this is in accord with nature.

30. Speak, both in the Senate and to anyone you may address, with fitting grace but without pedantic precision. Use wholesome language.

31. The court of Augustus: wife, daughter, grandsons, stepsons, sister, Agrippa, kinsmen, household, friends, Areius, Maecenas, doctors, priests—the whole court is dead. Then pass to others, the death not of an individual but of a whole family, such as that of the Pompeys; and the inscription found upon tombstones: "The last of his clan." Reflect how anxious the ancestors were to leave one to succeed them, yet unavoidably there comes one who is the last, and so again the death of a whole clan.

32. You must build your life deed by deed, and be satisfied if each deed, as far as is possible, fulfills its own end. And no one can prevent you from doing so. "But some external obstacle will bar the way." Nothing can bar your way to acting justly, temperately, rationally. "But some other effective action may be prevented." By cheerfully accepting that very obstacle and reasonably turning to what is possible, you will straightway find another action to perform which will fit in with the building of your life which we are discussing.

33. Accept without conceit, relinquish without reluctance.

34. If you ever saw a severed hand or foot, or a severed head lying somewhere apart from the rest of the body—that is what a man makes himself like, as far as he can, when he refuses to accept his lot and sets himself apart, or performs an unsocial act. Suppose you have torn yourself away from the unity of nature of which you had been born a part, and from which you have cut yourself off; yet here is the exquisite thing, that you may make yourself one with it again. This no god has

granted to any other part, namely, to achieve unity again after it has been separated and cut off. Consider the kindness with which he has honored man, for he has given him the power not to be torn from the Whole to begin with, and, after being cut off, to return and grow into unity again and to take up his assigned place as a part.

35. Just as the nature of the Whole has provided each rational being with his other powers, so we have received from it also this power: in the same way as the universal nature turns to its own purposes every obstacle that stands in its way, assigns it a place in the order of fate, and makes it part of itself, so the rational creature can turn every obstacle into material for his own actions and use it to attain his original purpose.

36. Let not the picture which imagination draws of your whole life disturb you, let not your mind concern itself with all the kinds of troubles which are likely to have happened in the past or are likely to happen in the future, but for each event as it happens ask yourself: what is there in this task which is a burden I cannot endure? For you will then be ashamed to confess that there is such. Then remind yourself that it is not the future or the past which weighs upon you, but always only the present, and that this present burden is lightened if you consider it in isolation, and rebuke your mind if it cannot stand merely against this.

37. Does Pantheia or Pergamus now stand by the coffin of Verus? Or Chabrias or Diotimus by that of Hadrian? [3] Ridiculous! And if they did, would the dead be aware of it? And if they were aware, would they be pleased? And even if they were pleased, are the mourners immortal? Are they too not fated to become old women and old men, and then to die? And what would the dead they mourned do after these had died? All this is but stench and gore in a winding sheet.

[3] For Diotimus see VIII. 25 above. Nothing more is known of him or of Chabrias. Pantheia was a concubine of Lucius (?) Verus.

38. If your eyesight is keen, look and judge most wisely, says he.

39. In the make-up of a rational creature I see no virtue in opposition to justice, but I do see self-control in opposition to pleasure.

40. If you pass no judgment about what seems to hurt you, you will yourself stand in greatest safety from pain. "What self?" The reason. "But I am not pure reason." Granted. Let not therefore reason take hurt to itself; if some other part of you fares ill, let it judge with regard to itself.

41. A hindrance to sense perception is an evil for the animal nature; a hindrance to desire is similarly an evil to the animal nature; and there is another hindrance which is an evil to the constitution of plants. So too a hindrance to the intelligence is an evil for the intelligent nature. Apply all this to yourself. Does pain or pleasure affect you? Sense perception will see to that. A hindrance arose to your desire? If you desired unconditionally,[4] then it would be an evil for the rational part, but if you accept the common lot, you have not yet been harmed or hindered. For no one else is wont to hinder the proper activities of the intelligence which remains untouched by fire, by steel, by a dictator, by abuse, by anything whatever, when it has become "a rounded sphere in solitude."

42. I do not deserve to hurt myself, for I have never yet willingly hurt anyone else.

43. Different people find joy in different things. I rejoice if my directing mind is healthy, avoiding no man or anything that happens to men, looking upon everything with kindly eyes, accepting everything and dealing with each thing on its merits.

44. Come, make the present time a gift to yourself. Those who rather pursue posthumous fame do not take into account

4 For the meaning of "desiring unconditionally" see V. 20 and n. 5. The quotation at the end is from Empedocles, and is quoted more fully at XII. 3 below, of the sphere of the universe (fr. 27).

that posterity will be the same kind of men as those whom they now dislike. Posterity too will be mortal. What is it to you anyway what words they will utter about you or how they may think of you?

45. Pick me up and put me down wherever you please, for I shall there keep my divine spirit propitious, that is, satisfied, if it is and acts in a manner compatible with its own nature.

Is this worthy, that my soul should, because of it, be in a bad way, deteriorating, humbled, yearning, fettered, and alarmed? What can you find worth this?

46. Nothing can happen to a man which is inappropriate for a man, nothing to an ox inappropriate for an ox, or to a vine inappropriate for a vine, or to a stone anything not proper for a stone. If what happens to each is both customary and natural, why should you protest? The common nature brought you nothing unendurable.

47. If you are distressed by something outside yourself, it is not the thing which troubles you but what you think about it, and this it is within your power to obliterate at once. If your distress is due to something in your own attitude, who can prevent you from correcting your doctrine? So too if you are distressed because you are not doing something you believe to be wholesome, why not do it rather than be distressed? "But there is too strong an obstacle in the way." Do not be distressed then, since you are not responsible for your inaction. "But life is not worth living if this is not done." Well, then, depart from life with good cheer, as he dies who has reached his end, and, at the same time, show good will to those who stand in your way.

48. Remember that your ruling spirit is invincible when it is withdrawn into itself and satisfied with itself, not doing what it does not wish to do, even if the stand it takes is unreasonable. How will it be then when its judgment is reasonable and prudent? That is why a mind free from passions is a citadel, and man has no more secure refuge to make him safe

for the future. He who has not seen this is stupid; he who has seen it and has not taken refuge there is unfortunate.

49. Do not to yourself add to the reports of your immediate sense impressions. You are told that so and so speaks ill of you. That is the report, but the report is not that you have been injured. I see that my little boy is ill. I do not see that he is in danger. Remain then within the limits of your actual perceptions; do not add to them from within yourself, and you are not affected. Or rather add to them as one who understands all that happens in the world.

50. A bitter cucumber? Throw it away. Brambles on the path? Walk around them. That is sufficient. Do not go on to say: Why do such things exist in the world? or you will be laughed at by a student of nature just as you would be laughed at by a carpenter or a cobbler if you criticized them because you see shavings and scrapings in their workshop from the things they are making. Yet they have a place to throw these things, whereas the nature of the Whole has nothing outside itself. The wonder of its art is that, keeping within its own limits, it changes back into itself all inside those limits that seems to decay, grow old and useless, that it makes these very things the source of new creations, so that it needs no substance outside itself and has no use for a place to throw decaying matter, but is satisfied with its own place, its own matter, and its own craftsmanship.

51. Be not slovenly in action or careless of the company you keep; let not your senses cause you to wander; not once must your soul contract with pain or leap with pleasure; ensure yourself leisure in life. "They kill you, butcher you, drive you away with curses." What matte·s this compared with your mind remaining pure, sound, temperate, and righteous? Just as if a man standing by a limpid, sweet spring were to curse it, yet the spring would not cease to bubble up fresh water; even if he throws mud or dung into it, the spring soon scatters this and washes it away, and is in no way stained. How then

may you possess such an eternally fresh spring rather than a well? By watching yourself at all seasons with a view to attaining freedom, together with kindliness, simplicity, and self-respect.

52. The man who does not know that there is an orderly universe does not know where he is; one who does not know the purpose to which the universe is by nature directed does not know his own nature or that of the universe. He who is without knowledge of any one of these things does not know for what purpose he himself was born. What kind of a man is he then, do you think, who avoids or pursues the noisy approval of those who know neither who they are nor where they are?

53. Do you seek praise from a man who curses himself three times an hour? Do you want to please a man who does not please himself? Can a man please himself who regrets almost everything he does?

54. Do not only breathe in unison with the air which surrounds you, but think now in unison with the intelligence which encompasses everything. For the intelligence which spreads everywhere and permeates everything is available to him who wishes to absorb it no less than air is available to him who is able to breathe.

55. All wickedness together does not harm the universe, nor does individual wickedness harm anyone else; it is harmful only to the wicked man, to whom it is given to rid himself of it as soon as he himself wishes.

56. To my will the will of my neighbor is as indifferent as is his life-breath or his flesh. Even though we have been born above all for each other's sake, nevertheless each of our directing minds has its own sphere of government. Else my neighbor's evil were my evil, which was not the god's intention, lest it be within another's power to bring misfortune upon me.

57. The sun appears to be poured down, and its light is poured in all directions, but it does not pour itself out. This pouring is but an extension of itself; indeed its rays are called

beams because of this extending in a straight line. You might understand the nature of a sunbeam if you observe the sunlight making its way into a dark house through a narrow opening, for it extends itself in a straight line, and as it were presses against any solid obstacle in its way which cuts off the air on the other side; it pauses there and does not glide off or fall off. Such must be the pouring and outpouring of thought, not a pouring out of itself but an extension; it does not press violently or furiously against any obstacles in its way, nor does it fall away from them, but it rests there and illuminates that which receives it. And that which does not receive it deprives itself of its light.

58. The man who fears death fears either a complete lack of awareness or awareness of a different kind. If no awareness, you will not be aware of evil either. If you acquire a different kind of awareness, you will be a different kind of creature and you will not cease to live.

59. Men are born for each other's sake. So either teach people or endure them.

60. An arrow moves in one way, the intellect in another, for even when the intellect is cautious and hovers around the object of its inquiry, it moves no less straight to its goal.

61. Enter into the directing mind of each man, and allow any other man to enter into yours.

BOOK IX

1. Wrongdoing is impious, for the nature of the Whole has fashioned rational creatures for each other's sake, so that they should benefit each other as they deserve but never injure one another. The man who transgresses its intent is clearly guilty of impiety toward the oldest of divinities, for the universal nature is the nature of ultimate realities, and these are closely related to all that now exists.

The man who speaks untruth is impious toward the same goddess, for her name is Truth and she is the first cause of all that is true. The deliberate liar is therefore impious insofar as he wrongs people by deceiving them, and the involuntary liar is also impious insofar as he is out of tune with the nature of the Whole and brings disorder as he struggles against the nature of the orderly universe. He who on his own initiative is carried towards the opposite of what is true does struggle against this. He received his original impulses from nature, and it is through neglecting them that he is no longer able to distinguish the false from the true.

And indeed the man who pursues pleasure as good, and avoids pain as evil, is impious also. He must needs reproach the common nature frequently for distributing something unfairly between inferior and good men, since inferior men often enjoy pleasures and possess the means to attain them, while good men are often involved in pain and in things that produce pain.

Then again, the man who is afraid of pain will at times be afraid of something that is to happen in the world, and this is already impious. Further, the pleasure seeker will not refrain from wrongdoing, which is obviously impious.

With regard to those things toward which the common nature is indifferent (for she would not create both pains and pleasures if she were not indifferent to both), those who would follow nature and be of like mind with her must also be in-different. Whoever is not himself indifferent to pain and pleasure or to life and death, or to reputation and the lack of it—things which the nature of the Whole uses indifferently —is clearly impious.

When I say that the common nature uses these things in-differently, I mean that they happen in due sequence and without difference to those who now are living, and to their posterity, and are caused by some long past impulse of Provi-dence. In accordance with this impulse and from a first prin-ciple Providence started the process which culminated in the present orderliness of the universe; for Providence had grasped certain rational, creative principles of what was to be, and marked out certain powers generative of substances, changes, and things of the same kind to succeed them.

2. It would be the part of a more accomplished man to leave the company of men without having tasted deceit, any kind of pretense, luxury, or pride; the second best is to breathe one's last after acquiring a distaste for these things. Or have you chosen to keep company with vice, and does not even your experience of it persuade you to flee from this pestilence? For the corruption of the mind is much more of a pestilence than the miasma and decay in the air which surrounds us.[1] The latter is a pestilence which attacks living creatures in their animal nature, whereas the former attacks human beings in their humanity.

3. Do not despise death, but find satisfaction in it, since it is one of the things which nature intends. As are youth and age, adolescence and maturity, growing teeth and beard and gray hairs, begetting, gestation, and giving birth, and the other natural activities of the different seasons of life, such too is dissolution. This then is the thoughtful human attitude to death: not exaggerated or violent or arrogant, but to await it as one of nature's activities, as now you wait for the time when

[1] This may be a reference to the plague which the troops brought back from the East and which decimated the empire for several decades.

the embryo will leave your wife's womb. Welcome in the same way the time when your soul will leave its present shell.

If you want a layman's rule which appeals to the heart, what will make you most easy in the face of death is to stop and observe the matters in hand which you are about to leave, and your associates' characters, which will no longer contaminate your soul. For, though one must not be offended by them but rather care for them and endure them with gentleness, yet remember that it is not from men who share your principles that you will be parted. This alone, if anything, would hold you back and make you cling to life, namely, if it had been granted you to share your life with those who professed the same doctrines. Now, however, you see how great a weariness there is in living with those who are out of tune with you, so that you say: "May you come more swiftly, O Death, lest I also may forget myself."

4. The sinner sins against himself; the wrongdoer wrongs himself by making himself evil.

5. One may often do wrong by omitting to do something, not only by doing something.

6. These are sufficient: a present thought which grasps reality, a present action socially beneficial, and a present disposition well satisfied with any happening due to an external cause.

7. Erase the impressions of sense and imagination, stay your impulse, quench your desire, withdraw your directing mind within itself.

8. Irrational creatures share in one soul, rational creatures each have a part of one intelligent soul, just as there is one earth of all earthy things, one light by which we see, one air to breathe for all of us who are endowed with sight and life.

9. All who have some quality in common tend toward that which is of the same kind. Every earthy thing sinks toward the earth; everything watery flows together, everything airy acts in the same way; so that these elements need to be kept apart by force. Fire is carried upward because of the elemental fire, but it is so ready to join with any fire flaring up here below

that every kind of somewhat dry matter is highly inflammable, because less of what hinders kindling is mixed with it.[2]

Further, everything which shares in a common intelligent nature tends similarly, or even more so, to that which is akin to it, for, as it is superior to other things, it is the more ready to mingle and join together with its own kind.

Right from the first, swarms, herds, nestlings being fed, and loves of a kind were found among irrational creatures. They already possessed souls, and in their higher parts an increasing tendency to unity which does not exist in plants or stones or timber.

Among rational creatures there are communities, friendships, households, and public meetings, and in war there are treaties and truces. Among still higher beings, though they are far distant from each other, there is union of a kind, like that of the stars. Thus a rise in the scale of beings brings a common feeling even among those who are far apart.

Behold what happens now. Intelligent beings alone have now forgotten the urge toward union with one another, and among them alone the flowing of like to like is not seen. Yet though they flee from it, it overtakes them, for nature is powerful. You will see what I mean if you observe carefully, for indeed you will sooner see the earthy out of touch with the earthy than man cut off from man.

10. A man also bears fruit, so does a god, and the universe,

[2] It was a basic principle of Greek physics that like attracts like and this was particularly applied to the elements, i.e., earth, water, air, and fire. Marcus states that this tendency of like to unite with like increases as we rise in the scale of nature: it is seen in animals who live in flocks, herds or swarms, and in the protection they give their young and their attachment to them, which is a kind of love. The tendency to unity is even stronger in rational creatures (i.e., men) and reaches its highest point among divine beings like the stars. Marcus often refers to the natural kinship among men because they share in Reason (e.g., IV. 4) and to this is due the origin of human societies. But the very freedom which reason gives can lead to evil as well as good and in degenerate times (such as Marcus believes himself to live in) men turn their back on the unifying principle to follow selfish ends. Ultimately, however, the sense of kinship and unity must prevail since it is in accord with the nature of man and that of the Whole.

each in its own due season. What does it matter if the expression is commonly used of vines and the like in its proper sense. Reason does bear fruit, its own and that of the Whole, and from Reason other things issue like unto itself.

11. If you can, teach them better ways, if you cannot, remember that you were granted kindliness for this purpose. Even the gods are kindly to such men, and co-operate with them to achieve some things—health, wealth, fame—so beneficent are they. You can be so too. Or tell me: Who prevents you?

12. Work on; not as one who is wretched, nor as wanting to be pitied or admired, but want this only: to act and desist as social reason dictates.

13. Today I left the troubles surrounding me, or rather, I cast them out. For they were not outside but within me, in my assumptions.

14. All things are the same: familiar in experience, ephemeral in duration, sordid in substance. All is now as it was in the time of those we have buried.

15. Matters outside our doors stand there by themselves neither knowing nor telling us anything about themselves. What then does tell us about them? The directing mind within us.

16. Good and evil for a rational social being reside not in passivity but in action, just as neither his virtue nor his vice lie in passivity but in action.[3]

17. For a stone that is thrown into the air it is neither evil to fall downwards nor good to be carried upwards.

18. Find your way into their directing minds and you will see what kind of judges you fear, and what poor judges they are about themselves.

19. Everything changes. You yourself are altering continu-

[3] Whereas the pleasure seeker finds his good in passively *feeling* pleasure. Cf. VI. 51 and n. 8.

ally and in some respects decaying. And so with the universe as a whole.

20. The wrong done by another you must leave with him.

21. The cessation of an activity, the ending of an impulse and a thought is, as it were, their death. There is no evil in this. Turn your thoughts now to the periods of your life: childhood, adolescence, youth, old age, for every change in these too is a death. Was this a dreadful thing? Now turn to your life with your grandfather, then to that with your mother, then to that with your father, and as you find many other destructions, changes and endings, ask yourself: was this a dreadful thing? Neither, in the same way, is the ending, cessation and change of your whole life.

22. Hasten to your own directing mind, to that of the Whole, and to that of your neighbor; to your own in order that you make it a just intelligence; to that of the Whole, that you may recall of what you are a part; to your neighbor's, that you may know whether he acts in ignorance or understanding, and reflect at the same time that it is akin to your own.

23. Just as you yourself complete a social system, so must your every action complete a life directed to social ends. If any action whatever of yours does not have this relationship, whether close or remote, to the social goal, it will break up your life and prevent it from being a unity. Such action is subversive, as is the man who in a community separates the part which is himself from the social symphony.

24. The tantrums and toys of children, and "little spirits carrying corpses," [4] make the story of visits to the underworld strike us more vividly.

25. Consider the formative quality of the cause, and contemplate this in isolation from the material element. Then

[4] An adaptation of the saying of Epictetus quoted at IV. 41 above, though no satisfactory explanation has been given why the realization that man is but a little soul encumbered with a body subject to death should make the stories of visits to the underworld, such as that of Odysseus in *Odyssey* XI, more striking.

mark off the longest time which the individually qualified thing is by nature intended to last.

26. You endured innumerable ills because you were not satisfied with your directing mind doing such actions as had been intended for it. Enough!

27. When someone blames you or hates you, or men express such feelings, penetrate their souls and observe what kind of people they are. You will see that you need not be anxious that they should think well of you. Yet you must be well-disposed toward them; by nature they are your friends, and the gods help them in all sorts of ways, through dreams, through oracles, at least to attain those things at which they aim.

28. The revolutions of the cosmos are the same, up and down, through the ages. Either the mind of the Whole has an impulse which reaches to each individual—and if this be so, welcome that which it set in motion—or it had this impulse once, and the rest has followed in consequence. Why then are you anxious? The Whole either is a god, and all is well, or it is without plan—atoms somehow and indivisible particles—but you need not be without plan yourself.

Very soon the earth will cover us all, and then the earth itself will change, and what it has changed into will also change indefinitely, and so on to eternity. As a man reflects upon these successive waves of changes and alterations, and their swift passing, he will despise all mortal things.

29. The cause of all things is like a torrent, it sweeps everything along. How puny are these little public men, wisely practical as they believe themselves to be. They are like children with running noses.[5] What then is a man to do? Do what nature now requires. Start now, if this be granted you; do not look around to see whether anyone will know about it. Do not expect Plato's ideal republic; be satisfied with the smallest step

[5] I have not followed Farquharson in transposing the clauses translated "How puny . . . noses" to come after the next three sentences. The transposition is unnecessary.

forward, and consider this is no small achievement. Who will change men's convictions? Yet without a change of convictions what else is public life but enslavement of the people who lament and pretend to be persuaded? Come now, speak to me of Alexander and Philip and Demetrius of Phalerum. I will follow them if they saw what nature required of them, and schooled themselves to this. But, if they played the hero, no one has condemned me to follow them. The work of philosophy is simple and modest. Do not lead me into arrogant pride.

30. Look down from heaven: innumerable flocks, innumerable ceremonials, varied voyagings in storm and calm, diversities among those who are born, associate together, and pass away. Consider the life lived by others long ago, the life to be lived after your time, and that lived now among primitive tribes; how many do not even know your name, how many will very soon forget it, how many who may praise you now will very soon blame you; reflect that neither remembrance nor fame is worthwhile, nor anything else whatever.

31. Imperturbability in the face of what comes upon you through an external cause; righteousness in activities caused from within you, that is, an impulse to act which culminates in socially useful actions—this being for you in accord with nature.

32. You can rid yourself of many superfluous troubles, for they exist wholly in your thoughts, and you will secure a large field for yourself by embracing the whole cosmos in thought, by reflecting upon everlasting time, and by observing the swift changing of each individual thing, how short is the time between birth and death, how vast that before your birth, how equally infinite the time after your dissolution.

33. All the things you see will soon decay, and those who witness this will soon themselves decay, and one who dies in extreme old age will be in the same position as one who dies before his time.

34. What kind of directing minds do these men have? What

things do they concern themselves with, what do they love and honor? Practice looking at their naked souls. When they believe that they hurt you with their reproaches, or benefit you by singing your praises—what conceit!

35. Loss is no other than change; this is a source of joy to the nature of the Whole and all that happens in accordance with it is good. These things have happened in the same manner from eternity and other such things will happen to eternity. Why then do you (when you suffer a loss) say that all that happened was bad and all will be bad in the future, that among so many gods no power has, it seems, ever been found to rectify them, and that the world is condemned to be afflicted with unending evils?

36. Corruption in the underlying substance of everything: water, dust, bones, stench. Or again: marble is the chalkstone of the earth, gold and silver its sediments, clothes are but hairs, purple but blood of a fish, and so on. And the vital breath is another of these things, it changes from this to that.

37. Enough of my wretched life, of mutterings and monkey tricks! Why are you perturbed? What is new in this? What upsets you? Is it the cause? Then look at it. Is it the substance? Then look at that. For apart from these there is nothing. But become, even now, simpler and better toward the gods too. To inquire into these things for a hundred years or three— it's all the same.

38. If he did wrong, the wrong is his. But perhaps he did no wrong.

39. Either all things come from one intelligent source and happen as in one body, and the part must not then complain of what is to the advantage of the Whole, or else all things are atoms and nothing but a medley and a dispersal. Why then are you perturbed? Say to your directing mind: "You are dead, you have decayed, you have been made a beast, you are an actor, you are joining the herd, and feeding like them."

40. Either the gods have no power or they have power. If they have not, why do you pray? If they have, why not rather

pray to be rid of fear and passion and grief for any of these things, rather than to have this and not that. In any case, if the gods can co-operate with men, it is with regard to these things.

But perhaps you will say: "This the gods have placed within my own power." Is it not better then to enjoy like a free man what is within your power than to be distracted by things you cannot control, like a lowly slave? Who told you that the gods cannot assist us even with what is within our power? At any rate, start praying for these things, and you will see. One man prays that he may sleep with a certain woman. You pray that you may not desire to sleep with her. Another prays to be rid of someone. You pray that you may not want to be rid of him. A third man prays that he may not lose his child. You pray that you may not be afraid of losing it. Fashion your prayers altogether thus, and observe what happens.

41. Epicurus says: "During my illness, my conversations were not on the subject of my bodily sufferings; I did not talk about that kind of thing to my visitors, but I continued my scientific discussions of the most important topics, indeed of this very point, namely how the mind preserves its imperturbability and protects its own welfare, although it shares the disturbances of the body. Nor did I allow my doctors to give themselves airs, as if their work was important, but my life continued its right and proper course." [6] Behave as he did, in illness if you are ill, and in all other circumstances. For it is a precept common to all philosophical persuasions not to abandon philosophy whatever happens, nor to join the ignorant and unscientific in their nonsensical chatter. Be concerned only with the duty of the moment and the means of doing it.

42. When somebody's shameless conduct offends you, ask yourself at once: "Is it possible for there to be no shameless men in the world?" It is not possible. Do not then ask for the impossible. For the man who asks for this is himself one of the shameless who needs must be in the world. Have the same

[6] This saying of Epicurus is preserved here only.

argument at hand for the knavish, the disloyal, indeed for every kind of wrongdoer. And when you remind yourself that such kinds of people must exist, you will also feel more kindly to them as individuals. It is also useful to have this thought at once: What quality has nature granted man to deal with this particular wrong? She has granted him gentleness as an antidote to deal with the headstrong, and other qualities to deal with others. You can, in general, teach one who errs to mend his ways, for every wrongdoer has erred and has failed to attain his real aim.

And how have you been injured? You will find that not one of those who have made you angry has done anything which will affect your mind for the worse, and your mind is the only place where evil or harm can come to you.

There is nothing evil or strange in a stupid man behaving stupidly. Ought you not rather to blame yourself for not foreseeing that he would go wrong in this way? Your intelligence gave you every reason to expect that he would probably err in this way, yet you forgot this and wonder that he did.

Most important, when you reproach a man for disloyalty or ingratitude, turn your thoughts upon yourself, for it is clearly your fault if you trusted a man of his disposition to be loyal, or if, when you granted a favor, you did not grant it for its own sake, so that it was its own reward. What more do you want when you benefit somebody, man as you are? Is it not enough to have acted in accord with your own nature, that you seek to be paid for it? As if the eye sought some return for seeing, or the feet for walking! Just as eye and foot were made for their own purpose which they accomplish by acting in accord with their own make-up, so man is by nature beneficent and acts in accord with his make-up and fulfills his own purpose whenever he grants a benefit or in any other manner contributes to the common good.[7]

7 For the thought of this passage cf. V. 6.

BOOK X

1. Will you ever, my soul, be good, simple, unified, in a pure state, more manifest than the body which surrounds you? Will you ever give proof of a friendly and affectionate disposition? Will you ever be fully satisfied, wanting nothing, desiring nothing living or inanimate for the enjoyment of pleasures, neither time to prolong your enjoyment, nor place, nor land, nor good weather, nor congenial company? You will then be satisfied with your present situation, and delight in all your present circumstances. You will convince yourself that everything which comes to you comes from the gods, that all is well with you and will continue to be so, all which the gods are wont to grant and will grant to insure the preservation of the Perfect Being which is good, just and beautiful, which begets all things, holds together and contains all things, which embraces what is being dissolved in order to generate other things of the same kind. Will you ever, my soul, be such as to co-operate with gods and men without reproaching them or being condemned by them?

2. Observe closely what your nature as a living being requires, since you are governed by the nature of mere life.[1] Then do it and welcome it provided your nature as a percipient animal is not the worse for it. Next, observe closely what your nature as an animal gifted with perception requires, and all this is to be accepted provided your nature as a rational creature is not the worse for it. Reason is indisputably social.

[1] Man's "nature as a living being" is what is elsewhere called the breath of life or life-soul, i.e., the lowest stratum of the human soul, which man shares with everything which has life. His "nature as a percipient animal" is in the percipient or animal-soul, the part he shares with animals; his "nature as a rational being" is the rational, i.e., specifically human part, the directing mind. Marcus is here more kindly than usual to the lower parts; at least they deserve care and attention, as long as the lower does not interfere with the higher.

Apply these rules and do not concern yourself with what is not your business.

3. Everything happens in such a way that you are by nature either able or unable to endure it. If it happens so that you can by nature endure it, do not complain but endure it as you are by nature able to do. If it happens so that you cannot endure it, do not complain, for it will anticipate your complaint by destroying you. But be sure to remember that it is within your power to endure anything which it is within the power of your thought to make endurable and bearable by representing it as to your advantage or as your duty.

4. If he falls into wrongdoing, teach him kindly, and show him what he overlooked; if you cannot do that, blame yourself, or not even yourself.

5. Whatever befalls you was prepared for you from eternity, and the interwoven sequence of causes was spinning your existence from all time, and this event as well.

6. Whether there be atoms or a natural order let it first be established that I am a part of the Whole, which is governed by Nature. Then, that I am somehow closely related to the other parts of the same kind as I. Keeping these tenets in mind, I shall not, since I am a part, be displeased with anything allotted to me from the Whole, for nothing injures the part if it is to the benefit of the Whole. The Whole contains nothing not beneficial to itself; all natures have this in common, but the nature of the universe has this further attribute, that it cannot be compelled by any outside cause to produce something injurious to itself.

Remembering then that I am a part of the Whole, and that the Whole is of this kind, I shall be satisfied with all that derives from it, and, being closely related to the parts of the same kind, I shall do nothing antisocial, but rather direct my thoughts to my kindred, direct my every impulse to the common good, and divert it from the opposite. While achieving this, life will of necessity flow easily, just as you would judge the life of a citizen to flow easily as he proceeds to benefit his fellow citizens by his actions, and welcomes whatever the city assigns to him.

7. All the parts of the Whole, by nature contained within the universe, must perish—this word to be used to signify change. If this were evil for the parts as well as necessary, then the life of the Whole could not be well conducted since its parts are ever on the way to change and are specifically constituted to perish—whether Nature undertook herself to harm her own parts and to make them unavoidably liable to evil, or whether she was unaware that such things were happening. Both assumptions are unconvincing.

If anyone abandons this concept of Nature and then explains that these things happen "naturally," [2] how ridiculous it is to say that it is natural for the parts of the Whole to change, and at the same time to be surprised and to complain as if this was something contrary to nature, especially as the dissolution is into the elements from which the things were made. It is either a dispersal of the component elements or else a change of the solid into earth and of the breath of life into air so that these are then taken up into the Reason of the Whole. And this remains true whether the Whole periodically returns to fire, or whether it is rejuvenated by perpetual changes.

Do not imagine that the solid and the airy in an individual

---

[2] Marcus here has in mind the Epicureans, who denied design and Providence yet recognized natural law—as indeed in Lucretius, Nature becomes almost a personified goddess. Marcus is here pointing out that on Epicurean as well as on Stoic principles, death is a natural process which we must not resent.

The last paragraph then points out that the material part of the individual, i.e., the body, has already changed many times since birth, yet somehow the individuality persists in life. He then mentions the possibility that the individuality is thereby so closely tied up with the material body that (as the Epicureans held) the individual "soul" is dispersed at death; this is irrelevant to the present argument which is not about personal immortality, but simply that death is natural and not to be feared, a point upon which Stoics and Epicureans, however much they differ on immortality, will agree.

date from his original birth, for he took in all this only yesterday or the day before as an inflow of food and as the air he
breathed. And it is this which he took in which changed, not
that to which his mother gave birth. Suppose that this new
material binds you too closely to the proper qualities of an individual thing: this assumption is not, I think, contrary to our
present argument.

8. Having claimed for yourself a name for such virtues as
goodness, self-respect, truthfulness, reasonableness, co-operativeness, and high-mindedness, take care that you be not called
by other names, and if you should forfeit your claim to those
virtues, return to them quickly. Keep in mind that "reasonableness" was intended to mean for you a discerning attention
to all things without negligence, "co-operativeness" meant the
willing acceptance of all that is allotted to you by the universal
nature, while "high-mindedness" meant the elevation of your
thoughts above the stirrings of the flesh whether pleasurable or
painful, above vainglory, death, and all other such things. If
therefore you keep for yourself a name for these virtues, without being greedy of their being attributed to you by others,
you will be a different man and enter upon a different life.

To continue such as you have been till now, to be torn
asunder and defiled in this kind of life, is altogether the part
of an insensitive man clinging to life like those who fight wild
beasts in the amphitheater, when, already half devoured, covered with wounds and gore, they yet beg to be kept alive till
tomorrow to be thrown in the same state to the same claws and
the same teeth.

Therefore set yourself on the path to those few virtues; if
you can stay with them, do so as if you had changed your
abode to some islands of the blessed. If, on the other hand,
you feel yourself falling away from them and you cannot master yourself, retire undaunted to some corner where you will
regain your self-control, or else depart from life altogether, not
in anger but simply, freely, and reverently. You will then have
achieved this one thing in your life at any rate, the leaving of
it in this manner.

In order to be mindful of those virtues it will be a great help to you to be mindful of the gods, and that they do not want flattery but wish all creatures endowed with reason to become like them, that the fig tree should fulfill the task of a fig tree, the dog the task of a dog, and man the task of a man.

9. Vulgar comedy, wars, excitements, torpor, servitude! Every day those holy doctrines of yours are obliterated, if you communicate their impressions to your mind without testing them by the knowledge of nature.[3]

One should observe every event and perform every action in such a manner that the duties imposed upon us by circumstances are fulfilled, and at the same time one's contemplative faculty is active, and the self-confidence which results from the knowledge of individual events is preserved, unnoticed but not concealed.

When will you take pleasure in simplicity? When in dignity? When in the knowledge of individual things, what each is in essence, what place it has in the universe, how long it is by nature meant to last, from what elements it has been put together, for whom it is available, who can grant it and take it away?

10. A spider is proud when it has hunted down a fly; one man, a hare; another, a sardine in his net; another, piglets; another, bears; another, Sarmatians. Are they not bandits, when you examine their convictions?[4]

11. Acquire a systematic view of how all things change into one another; consistently apply your mind to, and train yourself in, this aspect of the universe. Nothing is so productive of high-mindedness. The high-minded man has put off the restraints of the body; he realizes he must very soon leave the company of men and leave all these things behind, and he devotes himself to righteousness in his own actions and to the

[3] I.e., among the distractions of life you fail to check your mental pictures or impressions and your intelligence accepts them without examination; your doctrines thus not being exercised, then cease to live, as he puts it at VII. 2 (and see n. 1).

[4] For this section see Introd., pp. xiv-xv.

nature of the Whole in dealing with external events; he gives
no thought to what anyone may say or think about him, or
do against him; he is satisfied with two things: to be just in
his present action and to welcome his present lot. He has
given up all occupations and concerns which hindered his
leisure and has only one desire: to go forward along the
straight path according to the law and, in so going forward,
to follow the god.

12. What need of hidden meanings when you can examine
what has to be done? If you see your duty, go to it in a kindly
but uncompromising manner; if you do not see it, pause and
consult the best advisers. If some other factors prevent this,
then proceed cautiously according to your resources, holding
on to what appears to be just. For it is best to attain justice,
since any real failure is a failure to attain it. The man who
follows reason in all things is both a person of leisure and
prone to action, both cheerful and consistent.

13. Ask yourself as soon as you wake from sleep; will it
matter to you if just and good deeds incur blame? It will not.
Have you forgotten what kind of men they are at bed and
table who take pride in praising and blaming others, what
kind of things they do, avoid, pursue, steal and snatch, not
with hands and feet but with the most precious part of themselves which, when it wishes, is the means to loyalty, self-
respect, truthfulness, law, and a spirit of goodness?

14. To Nature who gives all things and takes them away,
the truly educated and reverent man says: "Give what you
wish; take away what you wish," and he says this not in a
spirit of recklessness but of obedience and good will toward
her.

15. The time left to you is short. Live it as on a mountain,[5]
for it matters not whether you live here or there, if one can

[5] The meaning of this phrase is obscure, but a comparison with X. 23
would suggest that "living on a mountain" means living the simple life,
away from the distractions of the city and the palace. If so, it is another
exhortation to live simply and in accordance with Stoic principles.

live anywhere in the world as in a community. Let men see, let them observe a true man living in accord with nature. If they cannot tolerate him, let them kill him. For death is better than to live as they do.

16. Do not discuss in general terms the question of what is a good man. Be one.

17. Let the whole of time and the whole of substance be continuously present to your mind, and that individual things are, as to substance, like a fig seed, and as to duration, like the twist of a gimlet.

18. Observe every object and realize that it is already being dissolved and in process of change, and, as it were, coming to be from decay or dispersion, and how each is born, in a sense, to die.

19. Consider what they are when eating, sleeping, fornicating, relieving themselves and so on. Then see what they are like when, haughty and violent in their seats of power, they rule over and chastise men. Yet how many needs they were just now enslaved to and for what reasons! And very soon they will have such needs again.[6]

20. What the nature of the Whole brings to each man is to his benefit, and it is so at the time she brings it.

21. "The earth loves rain; the proud heaven loves (when full of rain, to fall upon the earth)." [7] And the universe loves to create what is to happen. Therefore I say to the universe: "I join in your love." This too is the meaning of the phrase: "It loves to happen."

22. Either you continue to live here below and have now become used to it, or you withdraw from life and it was your

6 This passage has been misunderstood: Marcus is not, I believe, referring to "creatures who have risen to power from a servile condition," but making a simple contrast between the lords of the earth in their powerful official positions, and in their private lives when they are subject to the same physical needs as other men.

7 A quotation from a lost play of Euripides. The phrase "it loves to happen" is more natural in Greek.

wish to do so, or you die after doing your stint. There is no other alternative. Therefore be of good cheer.

23. Be always clear as to the meaning of the saying, "like this is yonder field," and how everything is the same here as on a mountain top, or on the seashore, or where you will. And you will clearly see the truth of Plato's words: "building about himself a sheepfold on a mountain," he says, and "milking his bleating flocks." [8]

24. What is my directing mind to me, what do I make of it now, and for what purpose do I now use it? Is it devoid of intelligence? Is it severed and detached from social association? Is it blended and mingled with the body so that it changes with it?

25. He who flees from his master is a runaway slave. The law is our master and he who transgresses against it is then a runaway too. The man who is grieved or angry or afraid wishes that something had not happened, were not happening, or would not happen, of those things which were ordered by that which rules over all, that is, the law which gives to each man what befalls him. It follows that the man who is afraid, grieved, or angry is a runaway slave.

26. The father casts his seed into the womb and then goes

---

[8] The first quotation (obviously incomplete) is unidentified; the second is from Plato's *Theaetetus* 174d-e. Preceding this in Plato is the famous description of how the philosopher seems foolish to the many because his thoughts are on higher things. Plato then says that the multitude's praises of despots and kings seem very silly to the philosopher, for despots and kings seem to him to be but a kind of herdsmen who effectively milk (βδάλλειν) a wilder and more treacherous kind of animal, namely humans. The philosopher thinks that kings and despots will be so busy doing this that they will inevitably become as boorish and uncultured as the herdsmen, just as the walls which surround them are (like) a sheepfold on the mountain (σηκὸν ἐν ὄρει τεῖχος περιβεβλημένον). Marcus does not quote exactly. The "words of Plato" he professes to quote are σηκὸν ἐν ὄρει περιβαλλόμενος and βδάλλων βληχήματα, but the reference is clear, and the thought is that the life of a ruler is as restrictive and as unsuited to philosophy as that of a shepherd on a mountain.

away; for the rest another causal force takes charge, fashions and perfects the child. From what small beginnings noteworthy things arise! Again, a man swallows food down his throat, and for the rest another causal force takes charge and produces sensation, impulse, life as a whole, and strength, and how many other strange things. Consider these things then which are thus done and hidden from us, and see the force which produces them, as we see that which weighs some things downward and makes others rise.[9] We do not see it with our eyes, but no less vividly for that.

27. Bear in mind continually how all such things as are happening now have happened before; bear in mind too that they will happen again, whole performances with the same scenery, all of which you know from your own experience and from earlier history. Keep these before your eyes; the whole court of Hadrian for example, the whole court of Antoninus, the whole court of Philip, of Alexander, of Croesus. For these were all of the same kind as now, only with different actors.

28. Picture to yourself every man who is pained or dissatisfied with anything as being like a pig kicking and squealing when sacrificed; and so is the man who laments silently, alone in his bed, that we are bound by fate. Realize too that it is granted only to the rational creature to submit willingly to the course of events; merely to submit is inevitable for all creatures.

29. Consider each one of your actions and ask yourself whether death is to be feared because it deprives us of this.

30. When you are vexed at another's wrongdoing, stop and consider what similar wrong you are committing, as, for example, considering money a blessing, or pleasure, or reputation, and so with each kind of wrong. If you think of this you

9 "That which weighs some things downward and makes others rise" is the principle which Marcus believed made, for example, earth sink to earth and fire rise. This, though we do not see it, obviously exists. So with those other causal forces.

will soon forget your anger when it occurs to you that the man is acting under compulsion, for what is he to do? Or, if you can, remove what compels him.

31. When you see Satyrion, think of Socraticus or Eutyches or Hymen, when you see Euphrates, of Eutychion or Silvanus, when Alciphron, of Tropaeophorus, when Severus, of Crito or Xenophon; [10] and when you look at yourself, think of one of the Caesars, and so in each case of someone resembling him. Then let the thought strike you: Where are those others? Nowhere, or wherever it may be. For in this way you will always see human life to be mere smoke and nothing, especially if you remind yourself that what once has changed is no more, forever. Why then be anxious? Why not be satisfied to spend this short life in a decent manner?

What kind of material circumstances and occupation are you fleeing from? What are all these circumstances but opportunities to exercise the reason which looks at life carefully and scientifically? Stay then until you have appropriated these things to yourself as a strong digestion appropriates everything, as a bright fire appropriates whatever you throw into it and from it produces flame and light.

32. See to it that no one who speaks the truth can say of you that you are not simple and good, and that anyone who thinks of you like that be a liar. All this is within your control, for who is there to prevent your being good and simple? You only have to decide to live no longer unless you are such. And if you are not, not even reason chooses that you should continue to live.

33. What is the soundest thing to do or say in these material circumstances? Whatever it is, do it or say it; do not make excuses as if you were being prevented.

You shall not cease from sorrowing until you reach a condition where it is as important to you to act in a manner

10 The text is somewhat uncertain. Nothing is known of any of these men, except Euphrates, Severus, and of course, Xenophon and Crito (see Biographical Index).

worthy of your human nature in dealing with the material circumstances which face you and surround you as luxury is important to the self-indulgent. For every action in accord with nature should be regarded as a delight. And you can act in this way anywhere.

It is not always given to a round stone to move in accordance with its own proper motion, nor to water, nor fire, nor any of those other things which are governed by an irrational nature or soul, for the obstacles which prevent them are many. Intellect and reason, on the other hand, can overcome any obstacle in their way, as is their nature and their wish.

Keep before your eyes the ease with which reason can make its way through all obstacles—just as fire rises, a stone falls, a round stone rolls down a slope—and seek for nothing further. The remaining obstacles are either those of the corpse which is our body, or they cannot shatter it or do us any harm without our judgment and the agreement of our reason itself.

Otherwise the man hindered would himself at once become evil. For in the case of all other organisms, whatever is harmed in any way becomes worse itself; but in our case, if one may say so, the man becomes better and more praiseworthy, if he makes the right use of his circumstances. Remember that, to put it in general terms, nothing harms one who is by nature a citizen if it does not harm the city, or harms the city if it does not harm the law, and none of the so-called misfortunes harms the law. And what does not harm the law does not harm either the city or the citizen.

34. Once a man has been bitten by the true doctrines, even the shortest well-known quotation will remind him to feel neither pain nor fear, as for example:

> Leaves by the wind are scattered on the ground;
> So with a human generation.[11]

11 The reference is to Homer, *Iliad* VI. 146-49. The whole passage runs as follows:
> As with a generation of leaves, so with one of men:
> These leaves the wind now scatters on the ground;
> Others will grow as forests bloom in springtime,
> And so with men: one generation lives, another dies.

Short-lived as leaves are your children; as leaves, too, the loud and loyal applause of your friends, and your enemies' curses, silent reproach, and ridicule; as leaves, too, are those who will hand on your posthumous fame. All these "grow at the spring season," then a breeze blows them down, and "the forest grows others" in their place. For all things have one attribute in common: they are short-lived, though you avoid them or pursue them as if they would last forever. In a short while you too will close your eyes in death, and he who carries you out to burial will almost at once be the object of another's lament.

35. A healthy eye must look at all that is to be seen, and not say: "I want soft colors," for so speaks a man suffering from ophthalmia. A healthy faculty of hearing or smelling should be ready for all sounds or smells, and a healthy stomach should be ready for all nourishment, and a millstone for all the things it was constituted to grind. And so, surely, a healthy mind should be prepared for all that happens. The mind which says; "Let my children be safe," or "Let all men praise whatever I do," is like the eye which requires soft colors, or the teeth which require tender food.

36. No one is so fortunate that there will not be some people at his death who will welcome this calamity. If he was earnest and wise, will there not be someone at the end who will say to himself: "Are we to be relieved of this schoolmaster? He was not hard on any of us, but I used to see him silently criticizing us." These things they will say of an earnest man, but how many other reasons there are in our case to make it a relief to be rid of us! Reflect on this when you are dying and you will depart more easily, thinking: "I am leaving the kind of life in which even my associates, for whom I labored, prayed and planned so much, are very willing to carry me to my grave, hoping perhaps for some relief from my death." Why then should one cling to a longer time here on earth? Yet do not for that reason feel less kindly to them as you depart, but preserve your usual self; be friendly, kindly, well-disposed. And do not go as one who is being torn from life, but as one who dies at peace as his soul slips away from his body; and so, too, leave

your associates. For it was Nature who bound you to them and associated you with them, and who now loosens the bond. I am thus set free as from kinsmen, but without protest or violence. For this is in accord with nature.

37. Acquire the habit, as far as possible, of asking yourself in connection with all the actions of men: "To what principle does he relate this action?" Start with yourself, and examine yourself first.

38. Remember that what pulls the strings is hidden within. It is the source of speech, it is the principle of life; it is, so to speak, the man himself. In your imagination never put this on a par with the containing vessel or the organs that are fashioned about it. These are but instruments like the ax, differing only in that they are attached. None of these parts is of any more use without the agent who moves or restrains them than the shuttle without the woman weaving, the pen without the writer, or the whip without the charioteer.

BOOK XI

1. The properties of the rational soul: it sees itself, it shapes itself, it makes itself such as it wishes to be, it gathers its own fruit, whereas the fruit of plants and what animals may be said to produce as fruit is gathered by others. The rational soul achieves its end at whatever point life may be cut off, unlike a dance, a play, and the like, where the whole performance is incomplete if it is interrupted; but in every scene, wherever it is overtaken by death, its intended task is completely fulfilled, so that it can say: "I am in full possession of what is my own."

Moreover, the rational soul travels through the whole universe and the void which surrounds it, and observes its form; it stretches into infinity of time and grasps and understands the periodic rebirth of the Whole; it observes that those who come after us will see nothing new, nothing different from what our predecessors saw, but in a sense a man of forty, if he has any intelligence, has seen all the past and all the future, because they are of the same kind as the present.

It is also characteristic of the rational soul to love its neighbors, to be truthful, to show reverence, and to honor nothing more than itself, which is also characteristic of the law. Thus there is no difference between the right Reason and the Reason embodied in justice.

2. You will come to despise pleasant songs, dances, wrestling and boxing, if you break up the melody into its individual notes and ask yourself in the case of each: Am I overcome by this? You will scorn to admit it. Proceed in the same way with every movement and posture of the dance. Altogether, except for virtue and the results of virtue, remember to look at once at the component parts, analyze them and despise them. And apply this same method to the whole of life.

3. What an admirable soul is that which is ready and willing, if the time has come to be released from the body, whether that release means extinction, dispersal, or survival. This readiness must be the result of a specific decision; not, as with the Christians,[1] of obstinate opposition, but of a reasoned and dignified decision, and without dramatics if it is to convince anyone else.

4. Have I done something for the common good? Then it has been to my advantage. This thought you must always keep before you, and never give up.

5. What is your vocation? To be a good man. This, however, can only come as a result of philosophic precepts about the nature of the Whole and the specific nature of man.

6. Tragedies were first produced to remind us of what happens, to show that this is how things naturally happen, and that you should not be vexed on the larger stage of life by

[1] This is the only reference to the Christians in the journal. For Marcus' general attitude to them see Introd., p. xxi. What we have here is a contemptuous condemnation of the emotional ecstasy which made many Christians welcome martyrdom. It is of course very natural that this ecstacy should be repulsive to the Stoic, who preached the rational control of all emotions. Those who would understand Marcus here should read his contemporary Lucian's satirical dialogue on "The End of Peregrinus," a Cynic philosopher who killed himself by leaping into a flaming pyre at Olympia at the conclusion of the Olympic games in A.D. 165 in order to teach men to despise death. This motive Lucian condemns as humbug; the man's only motive to him was a desire for notoriety. Peregrinus had been a Christian for a time, and Lucian's essay has some interesting remarks on the Christians too:

These wretched people (κακοδαίμονες) have convinced themselves that they will be immortal and live forever, which leads the majority of them to despise death and willingly to give themselves up to it. Then their first lawgiver persuaded them that they are all each other's brothers after they had once offended by denying the Greek gods; and they worship that impaled sophist of theirs and live according to his laws. They despise all property and hold it in common, accepting all this without any exact proof. So that if some charlatan and trickster comes among them who can profit by things, he can get rich in a short time by imposing on people.

And this is what Lucian represents Peregrinus as having done. However, it is Lucian's attitude to Peregrinus' death which is here especially relevant.

things which delight you in the theater; for you see that this is
the course they must take, and that even those who cry "O
Cithaeron" [2] endure them. Moreover, some things are usefully expressed by dramatic writers; in particular:

> My children and myself endure the gods' neglect.
> This too has reason to it.

And again:

> For what befalls should not arouse our anger,

and:

> Like ears of grain our lives are harvested,

and all other such sayings. After tragedy the Old Comedy was
introduced. Its freedom of speech had educational value, and
its very directness usefully reminded the spectators of the evils
of arrogance. With some such aim Diogenes too adopted the
same manner.[3] Reflect on the nature of the Middle Comedy
which came afterwards, with what aim the New Comedy was

---

[2] This exclamation, "O Cithaeron, why did you receive me?" is put in
the mouth of Oedipus at the end of Sophocles' *Oedipus King*. Cithaeron
is the mountain near Thebes where Oedipus had been exposed as a baby.
The quotation occurs in Epictetus I. 24. 16, a passage probably familiar
to Marcus, though the context is different.

The next three quotations are from lost plays of Euripides (see also
VII. 38-41 above).

[3] It was a traditional view that the Old Comedy, by its frank exposure
and condemnation of vice, had educational value (see Horace, *Satires* I. 4,
ad init.). Of this genre the comedies of Aristophanes are our only extant
examples. The division of Greek comedy into Old, Middle and New is
also traditional. The Middle Comedy was less concerned with social problems, and, according to Aristotle, was less frank and given more to innu-
endo (ὑπόνοια, *Nic. Ethics* IV. 1128a22), which the philosopher preferred.
The later New Comedy, of which Menander is our only representative,
was more a comedy of manners and had little concern for social problems.
It still ridiculed vice in individuals, but much less violently, and only for
dramatic purposes. Marcus' condemnation of it is purely on moralistic
grounds, social and moral criticism not being its chief aim—though we
may well doubt that it was the primary aim even of Aristophanes.

The Diogenes here referred to is obviously the fourth-century Cynic,
and Marcus means that his frank exposure of vice was of the same outspoken kind; in fact, he was celebrated for his shamelessness (ἀναιδεία).

introduced still later, and how it gradually slipped into mere love of the techniques of representation. One realizes that even these writers said some useful things, but what was the whole aim and purpose of this kind of poetry and drama?

7. How vividly you realize that no other condition of life is as conducive to philosophy as that in which you now find yourself.[4]

8. A branch cut off from its neighboring branch must of necessity be cut off from the whole tree. So a man who severs himself from a single other man falls away from the whole human community. The branch, however, is cut off by an external agent, whereas it is the man himself who separates himself from his neighbor through hatred or indifference, and he does not know that he has also cut himself off from the community of citizens. But there is this gift from Zeus, the founder of the society of men, that we can again grow at one with our neighbor and again help to perfect the Whole. However, if it happens too often, the separation makes the severed part hard to unite and restore again. The branch, too, which grew with the tree from the beginning, shared its vital force, and remained with it, is not altogether like the one that has been separated, whatever gardeners say.

Grow together, but do not share the same doctrines.[5]

9. Those who stand in your way as you proceed in accordance with the right Reason will not be able to turn you away from a healthy course of action; but neither should they be able to destroy your kindly feelings toward themselves. Watch yourself on both counts: not only that your judgment and actions be steadfast, but that you remain well-disposed to those who try to put obstacles in your way or otherwise annoy you. To be angry with them is just as much a weakness as to abandon a course of action or to yield through fear. Both are

---

[4] For this unusual sentiment, which contradicts Marcus' usual feeling about his position as emperor, see Introd., p. xvi.

[5] That is, recognize your kinship with mankind and remain part of it, doing what good you can, but be not affected by the beliefs of the majority.

deserters, the man who desists from action and yields to fear and the man who allows his feelings to be changed towards those who are by nature his kindred and his friends.

10. No nature is inferior to art, indeed the arts imitate the nature of things. If so, then the most perfect and comprehensive nature of all could not be inferior to artistic skill. All arts, at any rate, produce the lower for the sake of the higher, and so, surely, does nature. Hence the creation of justice among men; and from it all the other virtues spring. For justice will not be preserved if we are partial to things indifferent, or easy to deceive, or prone to falter and change.

11. Externals, whose pursuit or avoidance disturbs you, do not impose themselves upon you but in a sense you yourself go out to them.⁶ At any rate, let your judgment be calm, and they will remain still, and you will not be seen to either pursue or avoid them.

12. The sphere of the soul retains its own form ⁷ when it is not extended toward some external object, does not shrink within itself nor pour itself out, nor collapse, but is illumined with the light by which it sees the truth of all things, and the truth within itself.

13. Someone despises me. That is his concern. My concern is that I be not found to do or say anything which deserves to be despised. He will hate me? That is his concern; but I am kind and friendly to everyone, and ready to point out to this very man where he went wrong, not reproachfully nor to show off my forbearance, but genuinely and to benefit him, as the famous Phocion did, unless he was pretending.⁸

6 The meaning seems to be that these externals do not force themselves upon the mind and judgment because of passion or desire, or fear, but the mind considers them of its own volition and in its own good time, and should pass judgment without being disturbed by them.

7 For the comparison with a sphere, cf. VIII. 41.

8 When Phocion, the famous Athenian general, was condemned to death, he is supposed to have said that he bore no grudge against the Athenians for the potion of hemlock they were serving him (*Aelian* XII. 49). No reason has been found for Marcus' doubts about Phocion's sincerity.

The inner disposition must be such that the gods do not see a man angry at anything, nor complaining that he suffers. For what evil is there to you, if you are doing what is suited to your nature and accept the present as appropriate to the nature of the Whole, as a man straining to achieve what is for the common good.

14. Though they despise each other, they are obsequious to one another, and, though they want to outdo one another, they yield to each other.

15. How rotten and spurious is the man who says: "I have decided to be straightforward with you." What are you doing, fellow? You need not declare this beforehand; the facts will speak for themselves. It need not [9] be stamped on the forehead. Honesty is at once clear from the tone of voice and the look of the eyes, just as a loved one at once knows all from the glance of his lovers. The simple and good man must be all of a piece, so that anyone who approaches him will, whether he wants to or not, be as clearly aware of these virtues as he is aware of the stench of the unwashed. But calculated simplicity is like a dagger. Nothing is uglier than wolfish friendship. Avoid it at all costs. The good, simple, kindly man looks these qualities; they are seen at once.

16. To live the good life to the end. The power to do this is in the soul, if a man is indifferent to things of no importance. He will so remain if he examines each of these things both by analyzing it in its parts and as a whole, and remembers that not one of them creates a judgment about itself in us, nor does it force itself upon us.[10] The external things remain still; it is we who make judgments about them, and, as it were, inscribe them upon our minds, though we need not so inscribe them, and indeed we can erase immediately any such judgment which we have made without being aware of it. Remember further that the attention we give to such things is short-lived, and soon life will have ceased. What then is in-

---

[9] A negative seems to have dropped out of the text (probably οὐ after μετώπου) for the sense requires it.
[10] Cf. XI. 11 and n. 6.

tolerable in these things? If they are in accord with nature, rejoice in them and they will be easy to bear; if they are contrary to nature, find out what is in accord with your nature, and hasten to that, even if it brings you no fame, for every creature is forgiven if it seeks its own proper good.

17. Whence each thing has come, into what it is changing, what it will be when it has changed, and that it will suffer no evil.

18. *First:* What is my relation to other men; and that we were born for each other's sake; and, following the other principle,[11] that I was born to be their protector, as the ram is to his flock and the bull to his herd.

But start from this higher premise: if not atoms, then Nature governing the Whole; in that case the lower exist for the sake of the higher, and the higher for each other's sake.

Second: What kind of men they are at table, or in bed, and so on, but above all what compulsions their convictions have laid upon them. And these very actions, with what vanity they perform them!

Third: If they act right, we must not be vexed; if they act badly, they clearly do so involuntarily and in ignorance, for no soul is willingly deprived of truth [12] or of the ability to deal with each individual according to his deserts. At any rate, they dislike to be called unjust, unfeeling, acquisitive, in a word, men who wrong their neighbors.

Fourth: You frequently err yourself and are another of the same kind as they, that is, if you refrain from certain wrongs, yet have a disposition to commit them, or if you refrain through cowardice or love of good repute or some other such bad reason from the same kind of wrongdoing.

Fifth: You are not even sure they are doing wrong, for certain things are done as part of a plan; generally, one must first

---

11 Perhaps the principle that each man must fulfill his appropriate duty. There is a reference to the bull's proper function in defending the herd in Epictetus I. 2. 30.

12 Cf. VII. 63, and n. 16.

learn many things before one can judge another's action with understanding.

Sixth: When you are immoderately angry or impatient, remember that the life of man lasts but a moment, and after a brief while we have all been laid out for burial.

Seventh: It is not their actions which annoy us, for these lie within their directing minds, but our own conceptions of them. Eliminate these and be willing to discard your judgment that their action is dreadful, and your anger has gone. How shall you discard it? By realizing that no shame is involved for you. For, unless only that which involves shame is harmful, you yourself commit many wrongs and are a robber and a shifting character.

Eighth: How much harder to bear are the consequences of our anger and vexation at such actions than the actions themselves, which provoked our anger and vexation.

Ninth: Kindliness is invincible if it is genuine, not malicious or hypocritical. For what can the most insolent man do to you if you continue to be kind to him, and, if the occasion arises, gently advise him and unhurriedly teach him to change his ways at the very moment when he is trying to do you harm. "Don't, child, we were born for other things. I suffer no harm, but you are harmed, child, by such conduct." Then show him tactfully and in general terms that not even bees act like this, nor any creatures whose nature it is to live in herds. This should not be done ironically or reproachfully, but affectionately and without bitterness, not lecturing him, nor in order that a bystander should admire you, but for his ears alone even if others are standing near.

Remember these nine precepts as gifts from the Muses, and begin some time to be human, while you still live. One should guard equally against being angry with men and flattering them; both are antisocial and lead to injury. Have this thought at hand when you are getting angry: that violent feelings are not manly, but gentleness and calm are both more human and more manly; it is the gentle man, not one who is angry or hard to please, who has his portion of strength and sinews and courage. As such a character is closer to imperturbability, so he is closer to power; anger is a sign of weakness just as much as grief. Both have been wounded, and yielded to the wound.

If you will, accept also a *tenth* gift from the leader of the Muses, namely that it is madness to expect inferior men to do no wrong, for this is to desire the impossible. To agree that they wrong others, yet to expect them not to wrong you, is to be unfeeling and dictatorial.

19. Your directing mind may take four turns for the worse, against which you must be especially on your guard at all times. When you detect them, eliminate them at once, applying in each case the following formula: "This impression is not necessary, this one is antisocial, here you are not speaking your own feelings"—for to say what one does not feel is the height of absurdity. The fourth will make you reproach yourself because the more divine part of yourself has been defeated by and has yielded to your less honorable, your mortal part, the body and its gross pleasures.

20. Your breath of life and all the fiery part that is mingled in you, though by nature they rise upward, nevertheless obey the dispositions of the Whole and are held back here in the mixture that is your body. Further, all that is earth and water in you, though they naturally move downward, have nevertheless been raised, and stay in a position not naturally theirs. So that even the elements serve the Whole when they have been assigned a post, and are forcibly kept there until, also from the Whole, the signal comes for the relief of dissolution.

Is it then not a terrible thing that only the intelligent part of you is rebellious and indignant at the place assigned to it? Yet no force is brought to bear on it, only such influences as are in accord with its own nature. Yet it does not bear with this, and sets out on a contrary course. The tendency to wrongdoing, to licentiousness, to anger, grief, and fear, belongs only to one who has separated himself from Nature. Whenever the directing mind is indignant at anything that happens, then also it is leaving the post assigned to it, for it was made for piety and worship of the gods no less than for justice. For piety and worship of the gods are also essential to a good society, indeed are more venerable than deeds of justice.

21. "The man who does not have one single and constant aim in life cannot, throughout his life, remain the same man." [13] To say this is not enough, unless you add what kind of aim it should be. Just as there is not one and the same concept for all that most people in one way or another think is good, but only for one kind of good, namely the social good, so too the aim should be social and pertain to the community. For the man who directs all his own impulses toward this goal will make his actions also of this kind and he will, in this way, be always the same man.

22. The story of the mouse that lived in the hills, and the mouse that lived in town, and the excitement and agitation of the latter. [14]

23. Socrates used to call the beliefs of most people bogies to frighten children with. [15]

24. The Spartans at their festivals used to put benches for visitors in the shade, but they themselves sat anywhere.

25. Socrates' refusal of Perdiccas' invitation to visit him: "that I may not die the worst kind of death," that is, that I may not receive favors and be unable to return them. [16]

[13] The quotation has not been identified, but the idea that a man should remain the same, unaffected by the vicissitudes of life, preserving his inner peace, is common in Stoic writings.

[14] Originally a fable of Aesop (297); see also Horace, *Art of Poetry* 540.

[15] The word for bogey (*Lamia*) used here does not occur in Plato, but Socrates does refer to the fear of death as a bogey to frighten children (μορμολύκειον) in *Phaedo* 77e. This passage is referred to by Epictetus (II. 1. 25) and it is the reference in Epictetus which Marcus probably has in mind.

[16] Marcus is again quoting from memory. Aristotle tells this of Socrates (*Rhetoric* II. 23. 1398a24-26), but the Macedonian king is not Perdiccas but his son Archelaus.

26. In the writings of the Epicureans there is the advice to have in mind continually someone of the ancients who practiced virtue.[17]

27. The Pythagoreans tell us to look up into the sky at dawn, that we may be reminded of those realities which ever remain the same and accomplish their task always in the same way, of their order, their purity and their nakedness, for a star wears no veil.[18]

28. Like Socrates, girt in a loincloth, when Xanthippe had gone out and taken his tunic, and what Socrates said to his friends who were withdrawing in embarrassment when they saw him thus attired.[19]

29. In writing and in reading you must be a pupil before you can be a master.[20] And this is much more so in life.

30. You are born a slave, you have no share of reason.[21]

31. And in my own heart I laughed.[22]

32. They will blame virtue, heap harsh words upon it.[23]

33. Only a madman looks for a fig in winter; mad too is the man who seeks to have a child when it is no longer granted to him.[24]

34. When kissing one's child, one should, said Epictetus, say to oneself: "You will perhaps die tomorrow." Ill-omened words

[17] This advice is attributed to Epicurus by Seneca, *Epistles* XI. 8.

[18] Cf. VII. 47.

[19] This story is unknown.

[20] The saying derives ultimately from Solon (Diog. Laertius I. 60) ἄρχε πρῶτον μαθὼν ἄρχεσθαι.

[21] The reference is not known, but the truth of the statement is denied by Aristotle, *Politics* I. 13, 1260b5.

[22] The quotation is from Homer, *Odyssey* IX. 413: Odysseus laughs when the other Cyclopes withdraw, as Polyphemus had told them that "Nobody" is killing him. What Marcus has in mind in quoting it is impossible for us to guess.

[23] An inexact quotation from Hesiod, *Works and Days* 186, where the word ἀρετή (virtue) does not occur in the original. Hesiod has "they blame them [i.e., their aging parents] with harsh words."

[24] All the quotations in sections 33 to 38 are from Epictetus III. 84, 86-93 and III. 17-21, 22, 105.

these! "No word is ill-omened," he said, "which signifies a natural process. Else it would be ill-omened to say that the wheat has been harvested."

35. Grapes unripe, ripe, dried. Everything changes, not into nothingness, but into that which now is nothing.

36. No one can rob you of freedom of choice, as Epictetus says.

37. "One must," he said, "discover an art of assent, and on the question of impulses be always on the lookout that they should be indulged only conditionally, that they be directed to the social good, and that their strength be in proportion to the value of their ends; one must also keep altogether free from desire, and not be deflected toward anything that is not within our control."

38. "The contest is not just about a trifling subject, but about madness or sanity."

39. Socrates used to say: "What do you want? To have the souls of rational or irrational creatures?" "Of rational creatures." "What kind of rational creatures, healthy or weak?" "Healthy." "Why then don't you try to get them?" "Because we have them." "Then why do you fight, why are you at odds." [25]

[25] This Socratic extract cannot be identified.

BOOK XII

1. All those things, which you pray you may secure after a time, you can possess right now if you do not grudge them to yourself, that is, if you cease to think of the past, leave the future to Providence, and only redirect the present on the path to piety and justice: to piety, that you may regard your lot with affection, for nature brought it to you and you to it; to justice, that you may, freely and without prevarication, speak the truth and do what is in accord with the law and the worth of things. Be not impeded by another's wickedness, his ideas, his utterances, and certainly not by the sensations of that flesh which has grown around you. Let them be the concern of the body which feels them. If, when you at last come to make your exit, leaving all other things out of account, you prize only your directing mind and the divine within you, and are not afraid of ceasing to live, but are afraid of never beginning to live in accord with nature, then you will be a man worthy of the universe which created you. You will cease to be a stranger in your own country, surprised by the unexpectedness of day-to-day happenings, and ever dependent on this and that.

2. The god sees all the directing minds of men stripped of their material vessels, husks, and impurities, for it is with intelligence alone that he is in touch, with what has flowed out of him and been channelled into them. If you too accustom yourself to doing this, you will rid yourself of the distractions which surround you; for a man who does not see the enveloping flesh is certainly not likely to occupy himself with clothes, house, fame, and such camouflage and theatrical scenery.

3. You are a combination of three parts: body, vital breath, and intellect. The first two are yours insofar as you must care for them, but the third alone is yours in the strict sense.[1] There-

1 Cf. X. 2 and n. 1.

fore, if you separate from yourself, that is from your mind, all that other people do or say, all that you have said or done yourself, all that disturbs you as likely to happen, all that belongs to the body which encases you or the life-breath which has grown with it and thus reaches you without choice on your part, and all that the external whirl causes to rotate—if you separate all this from yourself, your power of intelligence will be freed from the bonds of fate, pure and liberated, to live its own life doing what is just, desiring what is happening and saying what is true. If, I say, you separate from your directing mind what is linked to it by passion, what is beyond us in time, and what is past, you will make yourself, like the sphere of Empedocles, "rounded and rejoicing in its solitude." [2] Practice to live only the present which you are now living, and you will be able to live through to the time of your death in imperturbability and kindliness, and at peace with the divinity which is within you.

4. I have often marveled that every man loves himself above all others, yet that he attaches less importance to his own idea of himself than to what his neighbors think about him. At any rate, if a god stood at someone's elbow, or a wise teacher, and ordered him to speak aloud every thought or idea he had as soon as it was conceived, he could not endure this command for a single day. Thus we respect our neighbor's ideas about us more than we respect ourselves.

5. How did the gods, who ordered all things well and in a' spirit of kindness toward men, ever overlook this one thing, that some few among men who were especially good, who had made most covenants with the gods, as it were, and become familiars of the divine through pious deeds and the performance of many sacred rites—that when these men died they were not born again but completely extinguished?

If this is indeed the case, know well that if it ought to have been otherwise, then the gods would have done otherwise. For if it had been just, it had also been possible; and if it had

[2] For the "sphere" of Empedocles see VIII. 41 above and n. 4. Cf. also XI. 12.

been in accord with nature, nature would have brought it about. And if it is not so, then its not being so should lead you to believe that it ought not to be so.

You should yourself see that in these wrongheaded questions you are pleading a case with the god. Now we could not thus be arguing with the gods if they were not very good and very just; and, if they are, they would not overlook anything in the ordered universe being unjustly and unreasonably neglected.

6. Accustom yourself to doing even the things you despair of doing well. The left hand is useless for other tasks because it is not accustomed to them, yet it holds the reins better than the right. This it is accustomed to.

7. In what state of mind and body should a man be when overtaken by death; the shortness of life; the chasm of time before and after; the weakness of all matter.

8. Observe the causes stripped of their coverings; observe the objectives of actions: what is pain? what is pleasure? what is death? what is fame? who is not the cause of his own pre-occupation? how no one can be hindered by another; that everything is what we think it is.

9. When applying one's doctrines one should be like the boxer, not the swordsman. For the latter uses a sword, puts it away and takes it up again, but the boxer always has his hands about him and only has to put them up.

10. See things as they are, analyzing them into matter, cause, and end.

11. What an opportunity man has to do nothing but what the god will approve, to accept whatever the god allots to him as following from his nature.

12. The gods must not be blamed, for they do no wrong whether voluntary or involuntary. Nor should men be blamed, for they do no wrong that is not involuntary. So you must blame no one.

13. How ridiculous and how much of a stranger in the universe is he who is surprised at anything which happens in his life.

14-15. Either the Necessity of fate and an unalterable order, or a propitious Providence, or a random and leaderless confusion. If an unalterable Necessity, why do you strain against it? If a Providence which allows itself to be placated, make yourself worthy of divine help. If a leaderless confusion, be glad that in that surging flood you have within yourself a directing intelligence. If the flood is to sweep you away, let it sweep away your flesh, your vital breath, and the rest, but your mind it will not sweep away. The flame of a lamp shines and does not cease to cast its rays of light until it is extinguished; shall then the truth and justice and reasonableness within you be extinguished before your time comes?

16. In the case of a man who gives the impression of having done wrong, how do I know it was a wrong? And if it definitely is, remember he has condemned himself, which is like tearing one's own face.

A man who wants bad men not to do wrong is like one who would want the fig tree not to produce a bitter juice in its figs, babies not to cry, a horse not to neigh, and other inevitable things. What else can the bad man do, in his state of mind? If you feel fierce about this, treat his state of mind.

17. If it is not the right thing, don't do it; if it is not true, don't say it.

18. Let your impulse be always to look at a thing as a whole, what that object is yonder which makes a certain impression on you, and to explain it by analyzing it into its cause, its matter, its objective, and the time within which it must come to an end.

19. Realize at some time that you have within you something stronger and more divine than the things which cause your passions and which would rule you altogether like a puppet on a string. What is my thought at the moment? Fear? Suspicion? Passion? Something of that sort?

20. First, do not act at random, without relating your actions to an end. Second, do not relate them to any end but the common good.

21. Before long you will not be anybody or exist anywhere, nor will any of the things you now see, or anyone of those now living. For all things are by nature intended to change, to be altered and destroyed, in order that other things in their turn may come to be.

22. Everything is as you think it to be, and the thinking is within your control. Eliminate your judgment of the thing when you wish and you will reach calm, like a sailor who doubles a headland to find everything still and a waveless bay.

23. Any single activity which comes to a timely end suffers no evil thereby; nor does the fact that it has ceased bring any evil upon the doer of this particular action. Similarly, if the combination of all one's actions which is one's life comes to a timely end, it suffers no evil from its ceasing, nor does he who brings this series to a timely end suffer evil. Nature sets a time and a limit, sometimes it is one's own nature if one dies from old age, and generally the nature of the Whole, through the changing of whose parts the universe retains its youth and its bloom. All that is to the advantage of the Whole is always fair and seasonable. Hence the cessation of life is no evil to the individual, since, as it is not due to any choice on his part nor against the common good, it brings no shame either, but it is good if it is timely for the Whole, bringing benefit to it and benefited by it. For a man who follows the same course as a god is borne along by the god, and his own judgment leads him along the same course.

24. You must have these three thoughts ready to use: about your actions, they should not be without purpose, nor other than Justice herself would have performed; about external circumstances, they are due either to Chance or Providence, and one should neither reproach Chance nor accuse Providence. *Second:* keep in mind what each being is, from the time its seed is sown to the time when it acquires a soul, and from the acquisition of the soul to the surrendering of it; from what elements it was constituted and into what elements it will be dissolved. *Third:* if you were suddenly taken up into the sky

and thence looked down on human affairs and noted the trickeries involved, you would despise it as you saw at the same time the crowd of beings around you who live in the air or the upper ether. And as often as you were thus lifted upwards you would see the same things below: monotony, and shortness of life; and these are the objects of your vanity.

25. Throw out the idea you have of this, and you are saved. And who can prevent your throwing it out?

26. When you find something hard to tolerate, you have forgotten that everything happens in accord with the nature of the Whole; that the wrong done to you is another's concern; and further, that everything which happens has always happened so, and will so happen, and is happening now, everywhere; and again, how close is the kinship between a man and the whole human race, for they are a community, not of blood or seed but of intelligence.

You have also forgotten that the intelligence of any individual is divine, and emanated from yonder; also that nothing is anyone's private property: even his child and his body and his very soul come from yonder; also that every man lives only the present, and this only he loses.

27. Recall continually those who showed overwhelming anger, those who reached the heights of glory or disaster, of enmity or any other kind of fortune. Then reflect, where are all those things today? Smoke and ashes, legend, or not even that. Think of all this kind of thing at once: Fabius Catullinus on his country estate, Lusius Lupus in his town gardens, Stertinius in Baiae, Tiberius on Capri, Velius Rufus; [3] in general terms, a violent desire allied with conceit. How cheap all this effort! How much wiser to build on the materials provided by circumstance, and to make oneself a man of justice

[3] Fabius Catullinus may be the same person as the Fabius mentioned in IV. 50. We know nothing of Lusius Lupus, nor of Stertinius; Tiberius is of course the Roman Emperor. Velius Rufus is probably the same person to whom a letter of Fronto is addressed (Marcus Cornelius Fronto, Vol. II, p. 87 in "Loeb Classical Library"). He is there said to be an old man.

and self-control, a follower of the gods, and to do so simply. For the man who swells with pride at his lack of pride is the hardest of all to tolerate.

28. To those who inquire: "Where did you see the gods, from what do you deduce that they exist, that you worship them thus?" First, our eyes can in fact see them.[4] Then, I have certainly not seen my soul either, but I prize it. So too with the gods whose power I experience on all occasions; it is from this that I deduce that they exist, and I revere them.

29. To be safe in life one should see each thing for what it is as a whole, what is its matter, what its cause, and from one's whole soul do what is right and speak what is true. What else is left but to enjoy life by linking one good deed to the next with not the smallest gap between.

30. The light of the sun is one, though it is broken by walls, mountains, and countless other things. There is one common substance though it is broken up into countless bodies with individual qualities; one animal-soul, even if broken up into countless natures and individual surfaces; there is one intelligent soul, even though it appears divided. The other parts of the things we have mentioned, such as the life-breath and the objects without sensation, are not related to each other. Nevertheless, they are held together by a certain oneness and by the gravitation of like to like. But the mind has its peculiar tendency toward its own kind, joins with it, and its feeling of community is not broken.

31. What do you require? To survive? Or is it the enjoyment of sense? To follow impulse, to increase and then again to cease? The ability to use your voice, your mind? Which of these seems to you a worthy object of desire? If one and all of them are unimportant to you, then continue to the end to follow Reason and the god. But it militates against such a course to honor those other things and to grieve at the thought that one is deprived of them by death.

32. What a small part of the infinite abyss of time has been

[4] Marcus means the sun and the heavenly bodies.

divided off for each of us, for very quickly it disappears into eternity. What a small part of the whole of matter, what a small part of the whole soul, what a small clod of the whole earth you creep on. As you reflect upon these things do not imagine anything to be important except this: to act as your nature urges you to do, and to endure what the common nature allots to you.

33. How does the directing mind treat itself? Everything depends on that. The rest, whether objects of your choice or not, are all dead bodies and smoke.

34. What should rouse men most to despise death is that even those who judge pleasure to be good and pain evil nonetheless despise death.[5]

35. The man who considers that which comes at its due season as the only good, that to perform many actions in accordance with the right reason is the same as to perform a few, and that to look upon the world for a longer or a briefer period makes no difference—this man has no fear even of death.

36. Mortal, you have been a citizen in this great city, what matter to you whether for five years or fifty, for what is in accord with the law is equal for all. What then is there to fear if you are sent away from the city not by a dictator or an unjust judge, but by the same nature which brought you to it, as if the magistrate who had chosen a comic actor were to dismiss him. "But I have not played the five acts, but only three." "You have played well, but in your life at any rate the three acts are the whole play." For he sets the limit who was at one time the cause of your creation, and is now the cause of your dissolution. You have no responsibility for either. So depart graciously, for he who dismisses you is also gracious.

5 An obvious reference to the Epicureans.

GLOSSARY OF TECHNICAL TERMS

ACCORD. To live and act in accord with nature is the purpose of Stoic ethics. It requires man to accept his lot, to recognize the purpose of the universe and to serve it willingly.

AGREEMENT with nature. *See* Accord.

ASSENT (*synkatathesis*). The Stoics (like the Epicureans) insisted upon the reliability of sense impressions, but some impressions were clear, while others were blurred, as by distance, or obscure. It was for the mind to distinguish between them, and when the mind declared an impression to be clear, and therefore true, it was said to "assent" to it. Here error was possible, but the Stoic sage never made that mistake.

ATOMS. Whenever Marcus speaks of atoms he is thinking of the philosophy of Epicurus (in Roman imperial times, the main rival of Stoicism before Christianity). This was atomism, which denied any purpose or providence, was purely mechanistic, and insisted that everything was made of atoms which came together fortuitously (though, as Marcus points out, even the Epicureans had to admit the existence of natural laws).

CAUSE (*aitia*). The Stoics regarded Reason or Logos as the causal principle of things, and as such it is often contrasted with the material (i.e., undifferentiated matter or *hylē*) upon which Reason works. Actually, Stoics regarded even Reason as matter, though of a much subtler kind.

COHERENCE (*hexis*) is the principle which holds together inanimate objects such as stones, timber, etc., while living things at all levels are held together by the soul.

CONDITIONALLY. A man should always set out upon a course of action conditionally or with reservations, because he must not be disappointed if prevented from completing it by circumstances beyond his control. He will accept the new circumstances and adapt himself to them without resentment. *See* Introd., p. xiii.

CONFLAGRATION (*ekpurōsis*). From time to time the universe was reabsorbed into the divine rarified Fire which is the Logos. Then the cycle of life would begin again when this Fire was again differentiated into the elements as we know them.

CONTROL. It was a basic tenet of Stoicism that the attainment of inner calm and devotion to the Logos was entirely within the control of the individual, since it was quite independent of external circumstances.

DIRECTING MIND (*hêgemonikon*). The highest part of the soul is the human reason, which is a fragment of the Logos; as such it is spoken of as the inner spirit, or the god within, and as the mind which must direct all the actions of one's life.

GOD. The ultimate Logos or Fire or Reason which directs the universe is also called the god, or the gods. The Stoics admitted polytheism in the sense that the parts of the Logos in different portions of the universe could be differentiated as Hera in the air, Poseidon in the sea, etc., so that, in spite of their tendency to monotheism which equated the Logos with Zeus, they did not discourage the worship of the other gods but interpreted them symbolically.

IMAGINATION (*phantasia*) is the power to form images in the mind, and these occur as a result of our sense perceptions of events around us, or as a result of bodily desires. In themselves they are neither good nor bad until the mind makes a judgment about them. See VII. 2 and n. 1.

IMPERTURBABILITY (*ataraxia*). The aim of the Stoic is complete calm within the soul, which must seek to remain unperturbed by any violent emotion. See Introd., pp. 18-19, 23.

INDIFFERENT (*adiaphora*). Indifferent things are those which make no difference to a man's happiness or inner state of virtue. To the Stoic, this meant all external possessions and events, including health, wealth, and honors of all kinds. See II. 2, IX. 1 *et passim*.

LIFE SPIRIT or LIFE SOUL (*pneuma*) is that kind of soul which is possessed by all living things. See Soul.

LOGOS is used to indicate the divine Reason which rules and directs the universe. In ordinary language the word means speech, word, or expression, and also the thought expressed. Hence it is used for both the power of speech, which distinguishes man from animals, and for human, and hence divine Reason. This pervades the universe, and was identified with Fire, of a subtler kind than that which we know. The first words of the Gospel of Saint John, "In the beginning was the Logos," were clearly written under Stoic influence.

MATTER or the material principle is often contrasted with the agent or causal principle, i.e., Reason or Logos. Basically, however, the Stoics believed everything to be material, even Reason, and in this philosophical sense were thoroughgoing materialists.

NATURE. The nature (*physis*) of a thing or being is its innate tendency to fulfill the functions which the purpose of the universe intended for it. The nature of the universe itself (the nature of the Whole) is that divine purpose embodied within it.

POWER. It is entirely within the power or control of the individual to achieve the inner poise and calm, the imperturbability which is virtue. External circumstances which are not within his power should not affect him. *See* Indifferent.

REASON. For reason in the world, *see* Logos; for reason in man, *see* Directing mind. Marcus also occasionally speaks of the practical reason (IV. 4), which is an Aristotelian term and means that less exalted activity of the mind which decides upon the right thing to do in given circumstances.

RESERVATION. *See* Conditionally.

SELF-SUFFICIENCY (*autarkeia*). Man's happiness depends entirely upon himself, since it consists in understanding the nature of the universe and living in accord with it, an inner state completely independent of external circumstances or the actions of other men. *See* Introd., pp. 18-19.

SOCIAL good, social benefit. As man is part of a community, ultimately the whole universe, his actions must be directed toward the good of the community. For the implied contradiction between this aim and that of self-sufficiency, *see* Introd., pp. 18-19.

SOPHIST. The name was originally applied to the traveling teachers of the 5th century B.C. who supplied the demand for some form of higher education, especially in the art of speaking, so important in Greek democracies. In the time of Marcus, a Sophist is a professional teacher of rhetoric.

SOUL (*psyché*). Everything which lives has soul, but plants have only the lowest kind of soul, the breath of life, or life-spirit; animals also possess a percipient soul, i.e., capable of sense perception and physical desires; in addition to these lower strata of soul, humans also have a rational soul which is a part of the Reason or Logos which governs the universe, and this enables them to understand the purposes of this universal Reason.

VIRTUE (*areté*). The Stoic admitted the general Greek virtues of courage, moderation, and justice, but all these were but expressions in different fields of the essential virtue of wisdom, which consisted of understanding the Logos and being willing to serve it, an inner state of soul.

WHOLE. Marcus uses the term whole (*holon*) for the universe when he wishes to emphasize its unity, its harmony, and the fact that it includes everything that exists. Thus he frequently speaks of the nature of the Whole, meaning the universal nature or purpose.

BIOGRAPHICAL INDEX

AESCHINES THE SOCRATIC (fourth century B.C.). Companion of Socrates, author of no longer extant Socratic dialogues.

AESOP. Said to have been a slave in the sixth century B.C.; Greek fables were ascribed to him from the fifth century on. The collection we possess dates from the second century A.D., collected by Babrius.

AFER, Domitius. Famous orator, died c. A.D. 59. Amassed a great fortune but was unpopular because of his prosecutions.

AGRIPPA, Marcus Vipsanius (c. 63-12 B.C.). Put his military talents loyally at the service of Octavian, helped considerably in making him Augustus, and was one of the emperor's chief lieutenants until his death.

ALEXANDER OF COTIAEUM. Greek grammarian and scholar. An intimate of Marcus, he lived in the palace (I. 10).

ALEXANDER THE GREAT (356-323 B.C.). Son of Philip of Macedon, conquered all Asia as far as the Indus and greatly helped to spread Greek culture to the East.

ALEXANDER, the Platonist, of Seleucia. A famous Sophist whom Marcus summoned to Paeonia and honored with the title of Greek Imperial Secretary (I. 12).

ANICETUS. Mentioned by Marcus

as his *librarius* (his scribe or private secretary) in A.D. 143.

ANTISTHENES (c. 455-360 B.C.). Companion of Socrates and writer of philosophic dialogues. He is often regarded as the founder of Cynicism.

ANTONINUS PIUS. Adopted by Hadrian as his successor, was emperor A.D. 138-161 and adoptive father of Marcus. Had a peaceful reign and was an excellent ruler. For his character see I. 16 and VI. 30.

APOLLONIUS of Chalcedon. Stoic philosopher brought to Rome by Antoninus Pius to teach Marcus Aurelius (I. 8).

ARCHIMEDES (c. 287-212 B.C.), of Syracuse. Famous mathematician, many of whose works are extant. Devised clever machines against the Roman besiegers of Syracuse.

AREIUS. Stoic philosopher and friend of the Emperor Augustus.

ARISTOPHANES (c. 450-383 B.C.). The famous writer of comedies, of which eleven are extant, the only examples of the Old Comedy which we possess.

ASCLEPIUS. In Homer a mortal physician, but in legend the god of healing and son of Apollo. His cult persisted through the centuries and many miraculous cures took place in his temples.

ATHENODOTUS. Teacher of Fronto.

AUGUSTUS (63 B.C.-A.D. 14), Gaius Octavius. Nephew of Caesar and founder of the Roman Empire. After Caesar's death, allied himself with Mark Antony and M. Lepidus in the second triumvirate, later defeated Antony at Actium in 31 B.C., and established the empire while professing to restore the republic.

AVIDIUS CASSIUS. Died A.D. 175 after he had rebelled against Marcus Aurelius and had had himself declared Emperor at Antioch. He had been a loyal officer under Hadrian and Pius. Unable to prevent his death, Marcus treated the traitor's widow and family with great kindness.

BACCHEIUS. Nothing further is known of him beyond the reference in I. 6.

BRUTUS, Marcus Junius (85-42 B.C.), the murderer of Caesar, who had pardoned him for being with Pompey in civil war. Defeated by Mark Antony and Octavian at Philippi, he committed suicide. Hero of the later Stoic opposition.

CAEDICIANUS (IV. 50). Probably a contemporary of Marcus. We hear of a man of that name as imperial legate in Dacia about A.D. 123-140.

CAESAR, Gaius Julius (c. 102-44 B.C.). Shrewd politician as well as probably the most brilliant Roman general. Consul in 59; then received the province of Gaul; was member of the first triumvirate against senatorial obstructionism. After conquest of Gaul, crossed the Rubicon with his army in 49; defeated Pompey in civil war and established his personal rule in Rome. Murdered on the Ides of March 44. Author of memoirs on *Gallic Wars* and some books on *Civil War*. A writer of clear and limpid style.

CAMILLUS. The Camilli were a famous early Roman family. At IV. 33 Marcus probably has in mind the famous Marcus Furius Camillus, who saved Rome after the Gallic invasion of 387 B.C.

CATO, Marcus Porcius (234-149 B.C.), known as "the Censor." Rugged opponent of Greek influences in Rome and of the new luxury. Consul in 195 B.C., a sworn enemy of Carthage. A great orator and a writer, he published many speeches; his treatise on agriculture is extant. His old-fashioned writings were much prized by archaists like Fronto in the second century A.D.

CATO, M. Porcius (95-46 B.C.). Great-grandson of Cato the Censor, consistent opponent of Caesar and hero of the later Stoics in opposition to the emperors. Committed suicide after the defeat at Thapsus. Famous for his uncompromising rectitude (I. 14).

CATULUS. Stoic philosopher, known only from I. 13.

CHRYSIPPUS (280-207 B.C.). Third head of the Stoic School, after Zeno and Cleanthes. He was a voluminous writer and might be said to have been the codifier of the Stoic philosophy. None of his works has survived.

CICERO, Marcus Tullius (106-43 B.C.). Roman statesman, consul in 63 B.C. when he suppressed Catiline's conspiracy. Was the greatest Roman orator, and many of his speeches are extant. His works on philosophy which popularized Greek philosophy in Rome had a very great influence. His works on rhetoric embody his ideal of culture and education and preserved much of Greek rhetorical theory.

CLOTHO. In Greek legend, one of the three Fates.

COMMODUS, Lucius Aelius Aurelius. Son of Marcus Aurelius, who designated Commodus as his successor and made him joint ruler in A.D. 177. Sole emperor 180-192 when he was murdered. Weak and foolish, power went to his head and he became unbalanced and cruel.

CRATES (c. 365-285 B.C.). Cynic philosopher, lived the life of a wandering preacher, helping people as he went, and acquired a great reputation for kindliness. Wrote poetry, tragedies and letters; none of his works remains.

CRITO. Contemporary and friend of Socrates. In the dialogue named after him Plato represents him as trying to persuade Socrates to escape from prison.

CROESUS. Fabulously wealthy king of Lydia, c. 560-546 B.C., he was defeated by the Persians and his kingdom was destroyed.

DEMETRIUS of Phalerum (c. 350-283 B.C.). Governed Athens 317 to 307 on behalf of Macedonian king Cassander, then went to Alexandria where he enjoyed the favor of Ptolemy Soter. Also scholar and writer, friend of Theophrastus.

DEMOCRITUS of Abdera (c. 460-370 B.C.). Adopted the atomic theory of his master Leucippus and developed it. (Perhaps the story of his being devoured by lice may be due to an ironic version of the atomic theory.) Only fragments of his work remain, some of which, on ethical matters, seem to have little relation to his philosophy. Nicknamed the laughing philosopher.

DENTATUS (IV. 33), probably Manius Curius Dentatus, of the famous Roman family, the Curii. A Roman general of the early third century B.C., who defeated Pyrrhus, and by his victories helped considerably to establish Roman power over Italy.

DIO, Chrysostomus ("golden-mouthed"). Rhetorician and Sophist in sympathy with Stoic opposition, was exiled by Domitian in A.D. 82, and turned to Cynic philosophy.

Exile ended by Nerva. Eighty of his speeches are extant.

DIOGENES LAERTIUS (early third century A.D.). Author of *The Lives and Opinions of Philosophers*. No philosopher himself, but the book is of great value where we have no better sources.

DIOGENES of Sinope (fourth century B.C.). The Cynic philosopher who preached a return to "natural" life, to an extremely simple mode of living. He himself lived in a large, earthenware tub.

DIOGNETUS. Said to have taught Marcus painting; he evidently, however, had wider responsibilities (I. 6).

DOMITIA LUCILLA. Mother of Marcus, was very wealthy in her own right; her house was a center of Greek culture. She died some time between A.D. 155 and 161.

DOMITIAN, Titus Flavius Domitianus, son of Vespasian, brother of Titus. Emperor A.D. 81-96, when he was murdered. Impatient of the Senate's power, he made the imperial rule much more openly personal and autocratic. Became a cruel tyrant in Rome in his last years but continued to rule the empire vigorously and well.

EPICTETUS (c. A.D. 55-135). Stoic preacher, whose conversations have been preserved by Arrian. Born a slave but manumitted. Exiled from Rome with other philosophers by

Domitian in 89, he settled in Epirus. (I. 7.)

EPICURUS (c. 342-272 B.C.). The originator of Epicurean philosophy, which he taught in his "garden" at Athens, declaring pleasure the only good but preaching frugal and austere life (the static or lasting pleasure). Four of his letters explaining his philosophy have been preserved.

EUDOXUS of Cnidos (c. 408-355 B.C.). Famous mathematician and astronomer who derived a most elaborate system of concentric spheres to explain the movements of the heavenly bodies.

EUPHRATES (early second century A.D.). Philosopher, friend of Pliny the Younger and of the emperor Hadrian.

FABIUS (IV. 50). Probably the same mentioned in XII. 27 as Fabius Catullinus, who loved his country retreat. The Fabii were a famous family, but Marcus in these places seems to refer to men nearer his own time.

FAUSTINA, Annia Galeria (c. A.D. 130-175). Daughter of Antoninus Pius and wife of Marcus Aurelius. Later historians blackened her character, but there is nothing of this in the journals or the correspondence of Marcus, nor any reliable evidence.

FRONTO, Marcus Cornelius (c. A.D. 100-166). Famous Roman orator and rhetorician, teacher of Marcus and lifelong friend. Their correspondence is in part extant. Originator of the so-called *elocutio novella*, which puts great emphasis on the use of the right words, has an inclination to archaism and elaborate use of similes.

HADRIAN, Publius Aelius Hadrianus. Successor to Trajan by adoption. Emperor A.D. 117-138. Cultured and philhellenic, he was satisfied to abandon or consolidate Trajan's conquests. Traveled widely in his empire and was considered an excellent emperor.

HELVIDIUS PRISCUS. Son-in-law of Thrasea Paetus, also member of opposition group. Exiled by Nero, recalled by Galba, exiled again and finally executed by Vespasian (*c.* A.D. 75).

HERACLITUS of Ephesus (*fl.* 500 B.C.). Philosopher who stressed the flux of all physical things, the chief though ever-changing element being fire, the only constant being the balance of change.

HERODES ATTICUS. The richest of the second century Sophists, gave magnificent buildings to his native Athens and many other places. One of the teachers of Marcus Aurelius, he is, however, not mentioned among those to whom Marcus owes much in Book I.

HIPPARCHUS. Famous Greek astronomer of the second century B.C.

HIPPOCRATES (fifth century B.C.).

The father of Greek medicine. Many medical writings attributed to him are still extant.

JULIANUS (IV. 50). Probably refers to a friend of Fronto who is mentioned in Fronto's correspondence.

LEPIDUS (IV. 50). Probably refers to a near contemporary, but we do not know who he was.

LUCIAN of Samosata (born *c.* A.D. 120). Educated as a rhetorician and Sophist, but then became a writer of satirical dialogues in Attic Greek, of which about eighty are extant. An extremely witty and amusing writer, he could, however, be savage in his attacks on sham and pomposity.

LUCRETIUS, Titus L. Carus (*c.* 94-55 B.C.). Roman poet, author of the *De Rerum Natura* (*On the Nature of Things*), a hexameter epic on Epicurean philosophy in six books, which is extant. He follows Epicurus faithfully; he is also a great poet.

MAECENAS, Gaius (d. 8 B.C.). Early friend of Augustus. When the latter had established his power, Maecenas took little part in affairs and became a patron of letters, particularly of Virgil and Horace.

MARCIANUS. Philosopher, unknown except for reference at I. 6.

MAXIMUS, Claudius. Stoic philosopher, contemporary of Marcus, of whom little is known; he may have been a proconsul of Africa mentioned by Apuleius.

MENANDER (342-291 B.C.). The most famous writer of comedy at Athens in his day, and for us the main writer of the New Comedy, much imitated by the Roman comic writers of the second century B.C. A complete play of his, the *Dyscolos*, has recently been discovered.

MENIPPUS of Gadara. Cynic philosopher of the early third century B.C. Originator of the Menippean satire, a serio-comic mixture of verse and prose.

MONIMUS, Cynic philosopher, pupil of Diogenes in the fourth century B.C. He denied that there was any criterion of truth to distinguish dream from reality (II. 15).

NERO, Claudius Caesar. Emperor A.D. 54-68. The first five years of his reign were peaceful but he gradually withdrew himself from the better influences of his ministers, Seneca and Burrus, and became the cruel tyrant whose name stands for vicious cruelty in all modern languages. His "fiddling while Rome burnt" is probably a myth, but his persecutions, of Christians and others, were real enough. He was murdered in 68.

NERVA, Marcus Cocceius. Chosen emperor by the Senate when he was about 66, after the murder of Domitian, in A.D. 96. Well-meaning but ineffec-

tive, he adopted Trajan as his successor, giving him full power even before his own death early in 98.

PERDICCAS. King of Macedon, 450-413 B.C.; first an ally and then an enemy of the Athenians.

PEREGRINUS (*c.* A.D. 100-165). Cynic philosopher who was for a time a Christian. Little is known of him apart from Lucian's unfair picture of him in "The End of Peregrinus."

PHALARIS. Tyrant of Acragas from 570 to 554 B.C. His cruelty was legendary, in particular his habit of roasting his victims alive in a hollow brazen bull.

PHILIP of Macedon. Reigned 359-336 B.C., unified his kingdom and made himself master of Greece, which recognized him as its leader. He thus prepared for the conquests by his son, Alexander the Great.

PHOCION (fourth century B.C.). Highly successful Athenian general. After the defeat by Philip, he made great efforts to keep the peace with the Macedonians. He somehow allowed Cassander's Macedonian fleet to occupy the Piraeus, chief Athenian port; was condemned to death and executed.

PLATO (429-347 B.C.). Disciple of Socrates and teacher of Aristotle, founded the Academy which had a continuous history till all pagan schools were closed in A.D. 529. His philosophical dialogues are extant, the most widely read being the *Republic*.

PLINY, C. Plinius Caecilius Secundus, known as the Younger (*c.* A.D. 61-113), held various posts under Trajan. Many of his letters are extant, the most famous being on the treatment of Christians. Student of Quintilian and friend of Tacitus, he was a well-known man of letters in his day.

PLUTARCH of Chaeronea (*c.* A.D. 46-127). Philosophizing scholar and moralist. He wrote many essays on moral and literary subjects which are extant, as are also his famous parallel *Lives* from Greek and Roman history.

POLEMO of Laodicea (*c.* A.D. 88-145). A famous Sophist of the exaggeratedly eloquent Asiatic style. Two declamations of his survive.

POMPEY, Gnaeus Pompeius Magnus (106-48 B.C.). Highly successful general of the last generation of the republic, especially in the East. Member, with Caesar and Crassus, of the first triumvirate. Opposed Caesar after latter crossed the Rubicon in 49, and was defeated by Caesar at Pharsalus in 48. Murdered when seeking refuge in Egypt.

PYTHAGORAS of Samos (late sixth century B.C.). Mathematician and philosopher, founder of the Pythagorean School. Believed in the purification of the soul by intellectual training, and that the reality of things could be expressed in numbers.

QUINTILIAN, Marcus Fabius Quintilianus (*c.* A.D. 35-100). Spanish-born Roman teacher of rhetoric, author of *Institutio Oratoria* (*The Education of the Orator*), a definitive work in twelve books on Greco-Roman education, rhetoric, and theories of literature.

RUSTICUS, Q. Junius (I. 7). Roman nobleman who persuaded Marcus to abandon rhetoric for philosophy about A.D. 145. Consul in 163, and Prefect of the City *c.* 165, when he had Justin the Martyr put to death.

SCIPIO. The two great Scipios are Publius Cornelius Scipio (236-184 B.C.), who directed the campaigns in Spain and in Africa during the war with Carthage and finally defeated Hannibal at Zama in Africa, from which he received the title of Africanus; and Scipio Aemilianus (185-129 B.C.), the destroyer of Carthage in 146 B.C. and the central figure of the so-called Scipionic Circle of philhellenists in Rome.

SENECA, Lucius Annaeus (*c.* 5 B.C.-A.D. 65), one of the wealthiest Romans, minister of Nero, allegedly involved in conspiracy and ordered to kill himself. Writer of many philosophic treatises, letters, and of nine tragedies, all of which are extant. Criticized by Quintilian for his forced and flashy style.

SEVERUS. Mentioned in I. 14 as "brother" of Marcus, is as-

sumed to mean Claudius Severus, whose son married a
daughter of Marcus. Often
identified with a Peripatetic
philosopher of the same name
and time.

SEXTUS of Chalcedon. Stoic philosopher and familiar of Marcus Aurelius (I. 9).

SOCRATES (469-399 B.C.). Athenian
philosopher, insisted on the
need to define one's terms, on
self-knowledge, the identity of
virtue with knowledge, and
education by question and answer. Executed for atheism
and "corrupting the young."
Though he never wrote anything himself, a whole Socratic
literature arose after his death,
notably by Plato and Xenophon.

TANDASIS. Lecturer in philosophy (I. 6). Otherwise unknown.

TELAUGES. Was apparently sati-
rized in one of the Dialogues
of Aeschines the Socratic.
Nothing else is known about
him. A Telauges is also mentioned by Diogenes Laertius as
the son of Pythagoras.

THEOPHRASTUS (c. 372-288 B.C.).
Greek philosopher, successor
of Aristotle as head of the
Lyceum. His most important
extant works are On Plants,
and the famous Characters,
about thirty short pen pictures of various types of men.
His writings cover a wide
range of subjects.

THRASEA PAETUS. Publius Clodius
(I. 14), one of the Stoic Re-
publican oppositions, was con-

demned under Nero and committed suicide (A.D. 66).
Glorified by Tacitus.

TIBERIUS (42 B.C.-A.D. 37). Re-
luctantly chosen by Augustus
to be his successor, after several earlier choices had died.
Had a brilliant military career;
but Tacitus represents him as
a tyrant, and most sources indicate that he was an austere,
difficult and unpopular ruler.

TITUS, Flavius Vespasianus. Son
of Vespasian, emperor A.D.
79-81. Had a brief and generous reign which, however,
depleted the treasuries so carefully saved by his father.

TRAJAN, Marcus Ulpius Trai-
anus. Successor by adoption to
Nerva; was emperor A.D. 98-
117. Vigorous military leader,
strict but humane. Adopted
Hadrian as his successor. His
correspondence with Pliny on
prosecution of Christians is
extant.

VELIUS RUFUS. An older contemporary of Marcus Aurelius and
a friend of Fronto.

VERUS, Lucius (A.D. 130-169).
Adopted by Antoninus Pius
along with Marcus Aurelius
and declared co-emperor by
the latter on his accession in
161. Weak and pleasure-loving,
but loyal to his "brother,"
whose power he did not contest.

VERUS, M. Annius Verus, grandfather of Marcus Aurelius (I. 1).

VERUS, M. Annius Verus, father
of Marcus. Husband of Domitia Lucilla. Died A.D. 135.

VERUS, M. Annius Verus, name of Marcus Aurelius before his adoption by Antoninus Pius.

VESPASIAN, Titus Flavius Vespasianus. Restored peace to the Empire after the civil wars which followed Nero's death. Reigned A.D. 69-79, with careful and successful policies. Founded the Flavian dynasty.

VOLESUS. Family name of the Valerii, famous in Roman history. We cannot tell whether Marcus has a particular one in mind at IV. 33.

XENOCRATES. Disciple of Plato, head of the Academy 339-314 B.C.

XENOPHON (c. 430-354 B.C.). Friend of Socrates, country gentleman and soldier. Author of historical, Socratic and moral works, and also of the *Anabasis*, the story of the famous expedition of the ten thousand Greeks with Cyrus into Asia, and of their return after the death of Cyrus at the battle of Cunaxa.

ZENO of Citium (335-263 B.C.). The founder of Stoicism. Established at Athens the School of the Porch (Stoa). Highly dogmatic, he has been compared to an Eastern prophet speaking Greek philosophy.